MILLION DOLLAR BEDROOM

ALSO BY MATT DECOURSEY

Balance Me

MATT DeCOURSEY

MILLION DOLLAR BEDROOM

SCRAPPY LESSONS OF SUCCESS, SETBACKS, AND OTHER SURPRISES NOT TAUGHT IN BUSINESS SCHOOL

R̞B
Realist Books

B

Realist Books

7235 West 162nd Terrace, Stilwell, KS 66085

Text copyright © 2017 by Matt DeCoursey
Manufactured in the United States of America.

ISBN-13: 978-0-692-87393-9
ISBN-10: 0-692-87393-7
Library of Congress Control Number: 2017938930

CONTENTS

INTRODUCTION   1

SECTION ONE:
HELLO, MY NAME IS _____.

My Accidental Business   7

Now Is the "Worst Time" to Start My Business   8

Let's Incorporate   11

The Price of Undervaluing Your Equity   13

Understanding Your Path to Revenue   17

This Bedroom Can Fit Another Desk, Right?   22

Let's Get an Intern. No, Seriously.   30

How Do These Search Engine Things Work?   33

Basic SEO Practices You Can Do That Matter   36

The Long Tail   42

A Mad Scientist Is Born   43

A Conversation with Jaysse Lopez of
Urban Necessities   48

Section Two:
It's Always Sunny in Cebu City

The Outsource Formula   62

You Can't Compete with My Non-Compete   65

Time for the Buyout   70

The Second Jill   75

Time to Partner Up   78

Building an Online Army   82

Decision Time—All You Can Do Is All You Can Do 87

Paul, Angela, and Justin Bieber, Too!   88

Killed by a Panda   91

Learning to Adapt   95

Scaling Back Up with Repurposed Technology   96

Coin Toss Moment   98

Small Business Funding   99

Leverage   100

The American Express Gold Card   101

A Ball of Rubber Bands   104

A Smashed Phone, Some Cursing,
and the Feeling of "Oh Sh*t!"   106

Soapy Bubbles   108

Planning? What's That? 113

A Conversation with General Homes Founder
and CEO Jim Olafson 115

Section Three:
Lessons to Learn Before
Starting the Next Big Thing

Are There *Any* .coms Left? 125

And We Have a Winner 128

How Tall Is the Ceiling in Here? 130

The Startup Phenomenon 132

Is There Room in Here for All of Us? 132

Other Essential Things to Consider 138

How Long Does It Take to Earn a Dollar? 140

Do I Really Know What I Am Getting Myself Into? 141

A Conversation with Matt Watson, Founder of
VinSolutions and CEO/Founder of Stackify 145

Section Four:
Sticking Your Toe in the Pool

Creating a Cynically Optimistic Plan 165

A Final Note for Those Seeking Investment 178

Important Decisions That Can't Be Undecided   178

Determining Equity and Roles   179

Funding, Funding, Funding   180

The VC Experience   181

Smart Money vs. Not-So-Smart Money   182

You Will Determine Your Own Outcome   184

AFTERWORD:
AT THIS POINT IT'S UP TO YOU   187

GLOSSARY   189

ACKNOWLEDGMENTS   199

ABOUT THE AUTHOR   201

INTRODUCTION

Y OU MAY BE wondering what is *in* this so-called "Million Dollar Bedroom." It's probably not what you're thinking. *Million Dollar Bedroom* is the story of how—starting with nothing more than an American Express card with an $8,000 limit and an extra bedroom—I created multiple businesses that ended up generating MILLIONS in revenue and huge amounts of profit. (It's impolite to ask how much, or tell.) This was all done from my home, in shorts and flip-flops, or bare feet depending on the mood. I'm going to use my narrative as a way of inspiring and helping you possibly figure out how to do the same. As we go through this wild, stressful, joyous, and fabulous tale together, I'll provide invaluable information and hard-won insights that only an extremely small number of people could or would be able to share.

What I *am* able to provide is a realist's point of view when it comes to business. I'm prepared to teach you things that the professors in the top business schools don't know. Because they haven't done it.

I am also going to carefully define many of my attempted successes—which is a nice way of saying "failures." If I had someone to teach me all of the stuff I

1

will teach you, I know for a fact I'd have an extra big sack of cash. These lessons of failure are in many ways more important than the stories of success. Why? Because I'm hoping to help you avoid expensive mistakes. That being said, I like to begin all of my books with a little truth telling:

1) If you are expecting to get rich NOW, forget about it. It doesn't work like that. I would be full of it if I told you that within six months you would be a millionaire through using my surefire system. IT AIN'T HAPPENING!

2) You don't need money to start making money—just time and effort.

3) You need to be ready to try ten things, hoping that ONE will work.

Sorry, did that scare you off? If it did, you weren't going to make it anyway, so you're welcome. I just saved you a lot of time and probably money.

Still with me? Are you ready to build your own Million Dollar Bedroom? If so, let's give it a shot!

SECTION ONE:

HELLO, MY NAME IS _____.

L ET ME INTRODUCE MYSELF. My name is Matt DeCoursey and in 2017 I turn forty-two years old. I'm on my second marriage, both to women named Jill. I have two children with the second Jill, and live in the suburbs of Kansas City.

Over the years, I've attended five different colleges and now I'm technically a junior. Notice I said "attended," not "graduated." I have a strong track record of professional success despite my equally impressive ability to drop out of colleges. For eight years, I worked in the musical instrument business, starting in sales and, despite never having had a "real job" until the age of twenty-five, managed to become a regional manager of a large retail chain by the time I was twenty-eight. I did that for a few years, then moved to Washington, DC and helped another business open a few high-end piano stores. After a divorce, the housing meltdown, and a strong desire NOT to sit in a piano store all day, I worked as a regional manager for Roland, the world's largest manufacturer of electronic musical instruments. I did that for a few more years, then decided that I was tired of traveling. Once again, I quit yet another job that most people work a lifetime to get only to end up going back to school in Indianapolis. That's the last you'll hear about most of that time, but I am thankful for all of the great stuff I learned, the awesome people I met, and the cool cities I lived in or visited along the way.

That brings us to 2008 when I was spending A LOT of time wondering, *What happened?* I had managed to make decent money through my jobs and the rental homes I sold on the good side of the housing meltdown, but now I was watching every bit of it disappear. I still owned an expensive home on the bad side of the meltdown. All of that coupled with giving my now-ex-wife half of everything wasn't leaving much left. (By the way, she didn't even want me to buy those rentals that made us $120,000 in two years. I'm not bitter…anymore.)

So here I am, thirty-three years old and back in school. But this time I was feeling good about it, as I had the chance to attend classes prepping for the Kelley School of Business. For those of you who don't know about Kelley, it is without a doubt the greatest thing in Indiana if you are a resident. The Kelley School of Business, which is associated with Indiana University, typically ranks anywhere from #6–#10 for business schools nationwide. That's Ivy League caliber. In fact, it's actually higher than quite a few Ivy League business schools. Needless to say, I was pretty excited.

But by 2009, reality was setting in. I hadn't worked for almost a year. And not only was I running out of cash, but I was also amassing quite a bit of debt via student loans. You do have to pay those back by the way. I needed to figure out how to make some money. And fast. But starting a business was just about the furthest thing from a realistic possibility.

At this point in the story, I haven't built the Million Dollar Bedroom yet. In fact, I was considering renting that bedroom out for some extra cash. I'm really happy I didn't because I was about to accidentally walk into my first Internet dollar.

My Accidental Business

I'm sure some of you have heard of the band Phish. In my younger years, I was more or less a hippie who wore the same T-shirt and shorts for days on end, all the while being more than happy to play a little "Puff Puff Give" with his bros. Hey, I was twenty, give me a break. I mean, who knows, you might have Glamour Shots floating around somewhere. So anyway, I like Phish. Still do. It's music that moves me. Prior to 2009, Phish was on "hiatus." Whatever. But in 2009 they were back! Woo hoo! And coming to Indianapolis. Count me in. But the day tickets went on sale, the high demand—coupled with the fact that Live Nation just launched a new ticketing system that couldn't handle the demand—meant I didn't get any tickets. Lame!

The next day tickets went on sale for a different Phish show. I got a little carried away and bought sixteen tickets, figuring that I'd somehow trade them for the show I really wanted. Long story short I sold them on eBay and made five hundred dollars. Hmm. . .

Was *this* what I was looking for—the Hail Mary pass from the far recesses of financial hell? Maybe.

So now I'm thinking, man this is pretty cool. I can sit in front of my computer for a few hours a day and just buy tickets and then sell them on eBay and make money? I'm in!

Spoiler alert: I learned quite a few tough lessons over the next few months, as it really *wasn't* that easy.

MILLION DOLLAR LESSON: Buying things that are in short supply doesn't always mean demand to the point of people paying a premium. However, buying things that are in short supply that people are PASSIONATE about equals a big PREMIUM. Passion = Premium.

Despite a few setbacks, I kept on working away. And thanks to a very-little-known country pop artist (Who was it again? Oh yeah, Taylor Swift) I was able to keep on keeping on.

Now Is the "Worst Time" to Start My Business

So I found a little hustle to bridge the gap until graduation. But I still had a pretty big issue; I didn't have any real money. Sure, I made a few bucks here and there, but I basically had no cash and just one credit card left (without a nearly maxed limit)—making this officially the WORST TIME EVER for me to try and start a new business.

Cash flow is the lifeblood of any business, big or small. Without it everything starts to dry up like a houseplant you forgot to water. I found myself spending what I could and then having to wait for tickets to arrive—only to ship them back out and wait again for that delivery to occur. And ticket resale marketplaces don't pay you until you deliver. Overall, that was a fairly long cycle. I needed to find some more money!

Every Tuesday I'd play poker at my neighbor Josh's house. We became friends due to the Kansas Jayhawks flag I proudly flew from the front porch of my house in Broad Ripple, a trendy little bar district in Indianapolis. I had recently moved to Indianapolis and literally knew NO ONE. Josh, also being from Kansas, was nice enough to more or less take me in socially. I can roll solo but appreciated meeting someone my age, plus all of the people he knew. It is very possible that if I hadn't met Josh and his friends, I wouldn't be telling this same story.

Okay, so back to the poker games. I'm really not much of a player. I don't have the patience. However, a twenty-dollar buy-in was worth the entertainment. And after a few months, I got to know the rotating cast of participants. Overall, many were like me, but I seemed to be viewed as being a little bit different. I was, after all, the thirty-three-year-old back-to-school guy. That's only relevant because, as I started buying tickets here and there, I ended up telling them what I was doing. We all thought it was kind of interesting. In fact, one of the guys from poker was with me that morning I struck out so badly trying to buy Phish tickets.

Things continued to improve. "Hey guys, I made $500 this month selling concert tickets online," I shared. Then later, "Hey guys, I made $1500 this month selling tickets." A few of my fellow card players noticed, but it wasn't until the third month when I proudly announced, "Hey guys, I made *$4,000* this month selling concert tickets online!" that I truly started getting some attention.

Later that same night, after busting out in the card game and already having had a few drinks, another player and I made the brilliant decision to go to the bars and continue drinking. Okay, the decision to continue drinking was not brilliant, however the result of the conversation to follow was worth every bit of the next day's hangover.

While continuing to irresponsibly drink on a weeknight he said to me, "Hey, you seem like you are doing pretty well with this ticket thing. How about you take my American Express card and kick me 25 percent of the profit for the stuff you buy with it."

"Seriously?" I said. "What's the limit?"

"I don't know, fifteen grand or something."

Holy shit! I just drank my way into a deal that was about to more than double my buying power! "Hell yeah, dude! I'm in. Let's see what happens!" I said and ordered another round.

So roughly a month went by, maybe two, and I had not only significantly increased my own profits, but now I had also made a fairly decent amount for my buddy.

Hmm…maybe I need to start asking more *people if I can leverage their credit cards too.*

Josh had been so kind to me as a neighbor, so why not start there? Once I showed him how we could make some money, he agreed. And the greatest thing? He offered me *two* cards with big limits. So now, over the course of 4–5 months, I went from having an available credit line of $8,000 to somewhere near $60,000!

LET'S INCORPORATE

It's important to remind you that despite all of this ticket buying and selling, I'm still in school. That spring, summer, and fall, I was taking semester course loads of 18–21 hours of business classes, trying to hurry up and get back in the workforce. Which makes me really want to point out that, after years of success, I have yet to see *any* of those Greek symbols from statistics and economics classes in the real world. Business school, if you haven't been, is really great from the angle that it teaches you a whole lot of basic logistical stuff. In fact, that is one of the more valuable things you can gain. So there I was, every day, running through various scenarios in class regarding sole proprietorships, limited liability companies (LLCs), S-corps, C-corps, and so on. I realized that I probably needed to set something up, as my Million Dollar Bedroom was slowly being built.

Let's take a minute here to loosely explain the differences of these entities, their benefits, and why in my opinion some setups are better than others.

If you start a business of any kind, you are by default a "sole proprietor." This is the most basic form of business ownership. It is also the one that leaves you the most personally exposed. A "sole prop," as it is sometimes called, means that you are reporting your income for purposes of tax, but haven't really set up anything legal or official regarding your enterprise. There are millions of people that are "sole props" and don't even know it.

So what is good and what is bad about this option? The good part is the simplicity. You don't have to do anything to set it up outside of calling the IRS and getting a Tax ID Number or Taxpayer Identification Number (TIN), which you can even get them to give you on that same call. You also don't need to formally do anything to shut it down if you abandon the business. These business entities are okay for most *up to a certain point*, which we will discuss momentarily. Now here is the downside of the sole prop setup: It leaves you 100 percent open to anything dumb you do while running your business. In fact, it leaves you 100 percent exposed in general. What does that mean? Any liability, lawsuits, judgments, liens, ANYTHING are tied to you PERSONALLY! If you get sued, there is no layer of protection for you. "The Man" (also known as the banks, insurance companies, government, people you owe money to, people that might choose to sue you, really *anybody*) has a direct shot at your assets, including your home, car, cash, retirement accounts—and if you are married, the assets of your SPOUSE too.

As my business grew and I learned more and more about the different business entities, I felt the rising need to set something up. However, it really wasn't that easy. After all, I had built this blossoming business and was still financing it with credit cards owned by others. Should I have partners? How does that even work?

Knowing I no longer wanted to be a sole proprietor, I then dove into figuring out what was going to be the right thing for me and, well, my soon-to-be business partner.

The Price of Undervaluing Your Equity

If you have only partially been paying attention up until now, STOP! LISTEN! LEARN! This is one of those moments when I am potentially going to save you a ton of money.

One of the biggest rookie moves I see people make when starting a new business is not understanding equity, partners, and the value of either. First off, it's easier to disband from the person you are legally married to than to get rid of your business partner. I'm NOT kidding at all. It's true. And until you understand *why*, you probably shouldn't even consider it. Let me explain.

If you decide to have, choose, or require a "partner," then you are more or less marrying that person in a business sense. Why? Because similar to a marriage, both of you will bring X assets to the soon-to-be-legally-binding entity. This can come in the form of cash, equipment, and property—really anything that has some tangible value. Whether you choose to form a legal partnership, LLC, or some variety of corporation, you will now be combining your "stuff" into one pool, and then in exchange agreeing to now own a percentage of that pool.

So here I am, thinking, *I'm just going to do this until I finish school; this isn't going to last more than a year or two.* I'll explain later why that was a bad move. But first, let's keep things moving along here.

I had already excluded forming a "partnership," which is the equivalent of a sole prop, except possible for multiple people, because it didn't offer enough protection for me. That left an LLC or a corporation. At the time in school, I was learning a lot about "S-corps," which is a corporation with a specific type of tax election. If we want to get real specific, it is actually an election you take when filing taxes if you meet some specific requirements, like having less than one hundred total shareholders or owners and a few other details. So why did this sound so great? Because this format prevents "double taxation," and you don't have to be an accountant for that term to scare you.

Now before we get too far into this, let's talk about what a corporation is. A corporation is an entity that business owners can form either by themselves or together. Corporations are everlasting, meaning they don't die. Sounds weird, right? In a way it is, but in the end, it's not. In order to form a corporation, you need to do several things, some of which I won't be listing here, as there are a lot of intricate details that I'm not licensed to give advice about. So why would you form a corporation? For protection! How does that work? Well, you did just form an everlasting entity. So now the entity is the one liable for any lawsuits, fines, debts, creditors, and so on. Meaning, you can lose your business for whatever reason, but most of the time it is going to stop there. Creditors won't be able to cut deeper than what is in the business.

Who thought of this? I don't know, look it up on Google. But what I can tell you is that our government doesn't want you to be totally decimated on top of losing your business. If I'm allowed to be 1000 percent candid, it's basically how rich white people back in the day prevented themselves from being exposed to the possibility of no longer being rich white people. Sorry, I told you I would be really honest with you in the introduction of this book.

For these protective reasons, I chose to form a corporation with my buddy from the card table. Now earlier, I also mentioned this "S" stuff and double taxation. The "S" election for those that meet its requirements allows profits to "pass through" straight to the owner's tax returns without first being taxed. Yes, I'll explain further. Let's take any Mega Company—how about the biggest of them all, Apple. So Apple earns a whole lot of profit and must pay tax on it. Afterward, the company either chooses to retain those earnings or pay dividends. Those dividends are then paid to the "shareholders" or "owners" based on the number of shares they own. So when you own one share of Apple, you own something like .0000000001 percent (no idea about the accuracy here) of the corporation. Collecting that dividend, or profit, means you then again have to pay tax on this "income."

To circumvent this "double taxation" scenario, the "S" election allows profits—based on your ownership position in the company—to just slide straight through to your tax return, thus requiring only *one* level of taxation. This is why the IRS requires less than one hundred total shareholders in order for the entity to take an S election. That's so the Mega Company in all of its power and glory is still required to pay its fair share of taxes.

This next part is where I really messed up. Not even considering the possibility that I might own this business for a long time, or that it could, would, or even *might* become big, I sold 25 percent of my company for what ended up being around a $20,000 cash contribution. Then in order to get this money in the bank and to assure my soon-to-be partner that I didn't expect him to quit his day job, I signed an agreement stating that I didn't require him to do anything other than put that first cash in. To be fair, that rookie mistake was ALL ME. In my mind, this little business was just to get me through school. Later you will learn why this was not only a naïve but also an expensive misstep.

So using an online service and paying around five hundred dollars total, we formed a corporation. Unless you like paying lawyers a lot of money, these online services are good value. Forming a corporation or LLC isn't really that hard if you know what you are doing—

but most of us don't and it isn't worth the risk of missing something important. These online services, for what they charge, are a bargain. They ask you all of the questions that you need to answer, and then get everything filed with the right agencies and/or whatever the state you are in requires. Regardless of what entity you choose to form, please also get advice from someone other than me. I am not an accountant, nor would I ever want to be. I'm also not a lawyer, although sometimes I think I might like to be. Finding the right accountants, lawyers, and various professional services that businesses need is essential for building your own Million Dollar Bedroom. What these trained professions will do in a few hours might take you *weeks*—only to still end up doing it wrong!

MILLION DOLLAR LESSON: Don't try to do everything yourself. Find experts where useful and focus your time and energy on making money and creating revenue!

Now you've got a little insight about the different kinds of business entities you can set up. However, before you do anything, we need to discuss some of the common reasons that businesses fail.

Understanding Your Path to Revenue

One of the most valuable concepts and things to understand is YOUR PATH TO REVENUE. I'm shaking my head as I write this section. Why? Because this is so grossly misunderstood, ignored, and rarely even considered by most people. However, having an understanding of your path to revenue can be THE determining factor controlling your success or failure. So here it is…

MILLION DOLLAR LESSON: Path to Revenue = How long it will take you to earn your first dollar in revenue.

The very first question I ask ANYONE seeking my advice about his or her totally awesome app, idea, or business is "So what's your path to revenue?" But you have a brilliant idea, right? Something that will without a doubt change the world, double profits, and reduce expenses. I don't want to hear it. How long will it take you to put one dollar in the bank? And I don't mean YOUR money; I mean a client's money!

This is why your path to revenue is so important. When you're getting ready to start your business, whether alone or with a partner, you will have a finite number of resources. By this I mean CASH. If you want to sound smart the next time you're talking about this with someone, use the term "burn rate." Meaning, how long will it take to burn your existing cash without taking in a dollar?

MILLION DOLLAR LESSON: Always assume that everything will take twice as long and cost three times as much as you think it will. Not doing so puts you in a terribly risky position.

So back on this path to revenue. There are numerous ways in which people kill their dreams by not understanding this critical concept. Here are the greatest culprits:

You Think Your Idea Is a Lot Better Than It Really Is.

I don't want to squash your ambition or ingenuity, but please make sure that you have a really strong understanding of whatever idea, concept, or product you are planning. Whenever I hear people say, "If only 10 percent of people that need this will use it, I'm rich!" I ask if they have any idea of *how* to reach those people— or what it could *cost*. This isn't *Field of Dreams*. Just because you build it doesn't mean they will come.

You Don't Understand How Hard It Is to Get People to Spend Their Money.

Later in the book (Spoiler Alert), you will learn about my Internet startup, GigaBook. Since I want to teach you this truism now, all I can say is that getting people to spend any amount of money is A LOT harder than you think—especially when it comes to apps, software, or software as a service. If you are selling goods or products, it can be a lot easier, but in some cases, remarkably harder.

You Thought You Had Your Budget Figured Out.

This is probably the most common reason businesses fail in the beginning. I just told you to assume everything would take twice as long and cost three times what you thought it would. These wake-up call expectations are so you don't run out of money well before you thought you would. Often times, you have no clue about what you don't know until the moment you realize that you, in fact, don't know it. That is why I want you to think about EVERYTHING you need when you're planning; I mean until your head hurts like mine did the next day after the bar story I told earlier. Why? Because I drank too much that night. Oh, you mean why such a strict review of what you need to get started? Due to your inexperience, there is going to be a whole lot of stuff that you didn't even consider. Then, on top of that, any new venture gets peppered with a whole lot of "one-time" expenses. These could be many little things. Like a box of envelopes might last you two months, but do you have more than four envelopes right now? Do you own the right software, equipment, and so on? It can add up quickly.

You Think You Will Be Up and Running Faster Than You Actually Will.

This isn't a Million Dollar Lesson but instead a common sense one: SHIT HAPPENS. It just does, so anticipate it.

That leads us to the final concept you need to consider:

YOU ONLY PLANNED FOR SUNNY DAYS, ROSES, AND COTTON CANDY.

This occurs when your planning only includes success. Yes, that is what we are aiming for, but what are you going to do when the plan takes a detour? Are you ready for that? The thing I found annoying in business school was that they seem to want to teach you like this:

A to B to C to D to E to F.

So let me teach you how it usually happens.

A to B, then F broke E, and it really messed up C, which then meant you can't get to C, so instead you try for D, but D didn't show up that day, so you were forced to go to E. That seemed to work until you realized that you couldn't really get all of the way to E without having first been to B and C. This is just one example, but there are exactly one billion combinations of this scenario. And if you are the first reader to email me with all of them, you win a prize.

Okay, so now you have some stuff to think about. Please do! These are some of the most valuable lessons I can give.

This Bedroom Can Fit Another Desk, Right?

And we're back to the newly formed Broad Ripple Tickets Corporation located in Indiana! Business has been good; so good that I think I need another person to help. I was starting to sell a lot more, which meant I had to deliver more, which meant that I had more "receivables" to track. A "receivable" or "accounts receivable" or "A/R" is money someone or another business owes you. In my case, it was owed to me for sales I had already made (which I had yet to be paid for) since the delivery wasn't complete.

MILLION DOLLAR LESSON: Selling more means you will probably need to *spend* more. Understand that your budget should probably be "scalable," which means that it can scale up or down based on increases or decreases in your revenue. And make sure your budget includes the means to carry or finance your receivables. You won't always get paid NOW.

So all of this A/R, shipping costs, and, well, everything was really piling up. Better get some help, I realized. I started talking to my friends and found an interested party. And then we had *two* desks in the extra bedroom. I'm going to jump forward another month now and quickly say that it didn't work out. My now-former good buddy was majorly pissed at me afterward. Sadly, we were never friends again, and I'm pretty sure he still hates me. But I wouldn't know, as it's been eight years since we last spoke. Do you get my point?

MILLION DOLLAR LESSON: Don't hire your friends or family if you value the relationship. It's business, not Thanksgiving dinner. As a business owner, you will be forced to make tough decisions. And it's possible that your friends or family might not be great employees, meaning…well, you know.

Still needing help, I ended up hiring someone that was already in the house. Well, at least one day a week. Since I'm not really one to enjoy cleaning my own place, I had been using the services of a young lady that cleaned homes as a side job. Over a few months, I had gotten to know her and saw that she was a really hard worker. So I gave her a shot.

MILLION DOLLAR LESSON: If you get to the point where you hire help, find people that are GREAT at the stuff you AREN'T GREAT at. Not only will this make your life easier, but you will also find that you won't do stuff you don't like doing. Which means it otherwise won't get done.

At this point, with some extra help with the logistics, I felt free. I could simply focus on making money. Sweet! That's what I love doing anyway. However, I was about to accidentally, but still awesomely, make things more complicated.

Whether you figured it out or this is news to you, I have A.D.D. It's my greatest tool—largely because the hyperactive thing, if harnessed like I can harness it, becomes lightning in a bottle. This trait also means I like to explore lots of stuff. In this case, other ways to make money.

Overall, the one thing I learned in my previous life as a salesperson, sales manager, and then sales trainer was that the more eyes that see your product, the more likely you are to sell it. So in the process of finding these avenues, I found A LOT of websites that sold tickets. But it was really weird; they all seemed to have the same tickets for sale. Some websites even looked so alike it was hard to tell them apart. How could that be? It didn't make sense until I realized that I had just discovered "affiliate marketing."

MILLION DOLLAR LESSON: If you have NO money but you DO have a computer, you can start a business as an affiliate marketer right now!

What was happening wasn't that one hundred different websites had the same tickets for sale, but instead that a large number of ticket sellers were using a sales platform called TicketNetwork. Cool! What TicketNetwork (or TN) does is provide an actual network that sellers can use to help each other represent and sell tickets that aren't all owned by them. Let me explain. Tickets are expensive and there are usually around 90,000 live events scheduled somewhere at any given time. It is impossible to carry, obtain, or even keep up with that amount of inventory. And as I was beginning to learn, when people inquire about tickets, it seems like they always want what you don't have.

What TN did was run an Internet pipeline into YOUR website, therefore allowing you to show MILLIONS of dollars' worth of inventory even if you didn't own a single ticket. If someone bought the tickets through your website, then you needed to contact the actual owner of those tickets, buy them from them, then deliver them to your buyer. The delivery could even be done directly from the seller you contacted—and why not, they could easily print out a shipping label through the TicketNetwork system. This was honestly the greatest thing I had ever found! Not only did their "point of sale" (or POS) help track all of our sales, we also now had access to this entire great inventory to sell without needing to pre-own any of it.

There was only one problem. I DIDN'T HAVE A WEBSITE, KNOW ANYTHING ABOUT WEBSITES, OR EVEN KNOW A COMPUTER PROGRAMMER. Therefore, I did some light searching via Google, then picked up the phone and starting calling some local programmers. I talked to quite a few before settling on one that I liked and we got to work.

So remember that problem I was talking about earlier about having a business partner? Well, I was about to start a new business inside of my existing business, but our agreement said we needed to agree on what we invested in. Dang. Regardless, I got him to agree on trying out this new venture. But immediately I knew I had a BIG problem. I absolutely did not like asking someone else for permission. But the real problem was that I had accepted investment in a "ticket resale" company, not an online marketing company. I was concerned that my partner might feel like he had claims to other stuff I wanted to do in the future. It didn't really play out like that as you will soon learn; however, it was a very legitimate concern.

So here we go. We are ready to conquer the Internet in more ways than one! We figured out pretty quickly how to get TicketNetwork's plugin to run through our template and we were online after spending roughly $5,000. Bring on the sales!

Right?

No?

Where are the sales?

Does this thing work or not?

What I had just started learning is that it takes a lot more than a website to sell stuff online. So now what? Still not flush with cash, I needed to go back to my old playbook. But first, something else needed attention.

I was still a student and my grades were seriously slipping. Wasn't this business supposed to get me to graduation? *Not if you fail every class on the way, dude!* With fall classes coming up, I had some major decisions to make.

I'll work on that later; I need to make money now!

So I got back into sales mode.

There are literally unlimited avenues that you can use to advertise, market, or promote an equally unlimited number of things. Some of these channels, such as advertising, require money. But what if you don't have much? It means that you will need to work harder. You agreed to that in the introduction, so now I will reward you with an introduction to "grassroots marketing."

Grassroots marketing is anything you do to promote, advertise, or gain exposure for whatever it is you are selling. There are also a nearly unlimited number of avenues to explore here. One of the most notable grassroots platforms is Craigslist. If you haven't heard of Craigslist, then you probably shouldn't be getting into online marketing, as it quite possibly is as old as the Internet itself. My point being supported by the fact it looks EXACTLY the same as it did ten years ago. Anyway, you can post your ads online for free for most categories.

So we—meaning my one employee and I—started posting a few ads each day on Craigslist with links to pages selling tickets on our new website. We got our first sale on the first day we tried! SWEET! We were clearly geniuses. The tickets they bought (to see Blink-182, I think) came up to one hundred dollars total, plus a 12 percent service fee, then fifteen dollars for shipping. Man, this was great.

So let's do the breakdown.

The total transaction was $127.

Whenever you charge a customer's credit card, the "processing" company will charge you roughly 3 percent, so in this case $3.81.

The fifteen dollars we collected for shipping meant we had to purchase the shipping label. That cost $14.82. At least we made eighteen cents on that. WAIT! We had to pay 3 percent in credit card processing fees on that $15?! We *lost* money on the shipping label?!

In order to get the tickets, we had to make not one but two calls to the seller because they were "busy" the first time. Then it took us about an hour to learn how to create a "purchase order" or "PO" using our new POS system. A "PO" is the actual order you send to a supplier or a vendor with your order and payment information. Since my employee made fifteen dollars an hour, that cost me about fifteen dollars.

So let's do the math:
$127 collected
-$3.81 for credit card fees
-$14.82 for the FedEx label
-$15.00 in labor
-$100 for the cost of the tickets we needed to buy to fill the order
= -$6.63

Wait, is that right? We *lost over six dollars* making a sale that we charge a fee on? That can't be right. Run the numbers again. Yep! It's right; actually it's *worse*. We didn't consider that it took us another hour to post the ads that ended up generating ONE sale. AARGH!!!!

Clearly I had to make some adjustments. After a little investigation and research, we learned that we could in fact raise our "service fee" a little in order to cover the margin. However, the profit margins remained thin.

I wouldn't be doing a good job of teaching you the essentials of owning and operating a business if I didn't pause here and visit "margins."

Your **gross margin** is the difference between *what you sell something for* and *what you paid for it*. For example, if you sell something for $125 that costs you $100, your gross margin is $25. That certainly does not mean you made $25 of true profit because other factors come into play.

The **profit margin** is your sales minus costs. This includes the cost of goods and other factors like shipping. It is not uncommon to see businesses with large numbers in the gross margin column of their financial reports yet still losing money at the bottom line. It's all about expenses.

MILLION DOLLAR LESSON: Know your numbers, know your margins. This is a whole lot more than just the "cost of goods" or "COG." The cost of labor and your own personal time have value, as do any other resources or expenses you incur along the way.

Let's Get an Intern. No, Seriously.

As my business continued growing, so did my need for extra help. From my prior experience in the professional world, I learned firsthand the value of having the best people around. That's really a no-brainer. However, there is a catch. The best people want the best paychecks most of the time. They also value stability, benefits, and generally don't have a desire to work in the extra bedroom of your home. Therefore, I had to get creative.

One night during my weekly poker games, my neighbor Josh joked that what was going on at my house reminded him of an episode of *Seinfeld*—the one where Kramer, after starting his own business, Kramerica, adds an intern to his staff. Having always been a fan of the TV series, I went home later that night and re-watched the episode on YouTube. Wow! This might actually work, I thought. But would an accredited school actually grant an internship to the business operating out of my extra bedroom? I figured they wouldn't, but it was worth a shot.

When I went to class the next day, I stopped by the Kelley School of Business's Career and Internships office and grabbed whatever information they had. After reading the general criteria, I couldn't see why my business wouldn't qualify. Just to make sure, I sent an email to the office. Not only did we qualify, but apparently we were one of the only online or ecommerce operations that would have open positions. Keep in mind this was 2009—the Internet was still blossoming in many ways. So I went ahead and set up an internship opportunity, posted it online, then went to bed.

The next day I checked for applicants. You've gotta be kidding me! Dozens! Record keeping wasn't really my strong suit at the time, but I can confidently say that when I turned the ad off a few days later, the intern applicants roughly totaled seventy-five. And as I perused the applications, I was doubly shocked. All of them were students either currently enrolled in the Kelley School or about to be. These were really smart kids! Having quite a bit of experience with hiring, I knew that I had to reduce this huge pool of candidates.

MILLION DOLLAR LESSON: When people apply for a position, if they can't do a professional job in presenting a resume, then they aren't going to do a professional job when they show up for Day One.

I immediately removed all of what I like to call "crapplications." By this, I mean the ones that clearly did a poor job of presenting themselves or selling their own worth. How? Start by removing the resumes that were created with little to no evident care. If applicants can't reasonably relay a message to you about themselves, then they aren't going to do any better when they relay messages on behalf of your company to your clients. Then, if you still have too deep of a pool, start looking for those with personal achievements that make them stand out. By this, I mean those doing more than the regular person. I personally like hiring people who have a history of playing TEAM sports. This means that they are aware of the concept of teamwork, but more importantly are probably used to getting feedback or coaching.

Following this criterion, I got the resume pile down to about 10–12 potential interns. Next, I sent each an introductory email requesting a phone interview. Now *this* is an important step in the process. I'm about to save you quite a bit of time.

MILLION DOLLAR LESSON: When interviewing candidates for open positions, always request a phone interview first. You will find that you eliminate half of the candidates during this process. It will save you a huge amount of time and effort.

From the dozen or so introductory emails I sent, I got about 7–8 responses and set up times to chat on the phone. *Bam!* After the phone interviews, I'm down to four viable candidates, and I schedule in-person interviews. One doesn't even show up. Three good people left. The first two interviews are with candidates who I just don't see myself working with, especially in my own home. Feeling a little discouraged, and mildly questioning my applicant-thinning process, I awaited the arrival of my third interview. *Knock knock.* I open the door and find a young man, immediately personable and confident. After a very short get-to-know-you period, I ask one of my favorite interview questions:

When you are working at any given time, what do you prefer to be doing the most?

Generally, you are looking for a response like, "Whatever the most important task is." Or "Whatever needs to be done."

I received what is still very much the best answer I've ever heard: "Whatever makes us the most money!"

No hesitation, no thought needed. *I was sure we found our guy!*

Now that all being said, here is another lesson that can save you a hell of a lot of heartache!

MILLION DOLLAR LESSON: Always, no matter how much you like an applicant, interview them three different times, on three different days, and if possible, let them talk to three different people. What you love one day you might find really annoying on the next. The person you think is great might clearly be a losing bet in the eyes of another.

After a few more meetings, our newest addition to the Million Dollar Bedroom was onboard. Not to spoil any later parts of the story, but this same team member ended up working with us for YEARS and was a big part of our success. Case in point, a solid and thorough hiring process really pays off.

How Do These Search Engine Things Work?

Now that we were diving headfirst into the world of e-commerce, it was necessary to learn more about search engines, including Google, Yahoo, Bing, and whatever else you might want to add. First off, you will eventually meet someone who claims to be an SEO expert. SEO stands for Search Engine Optimization, or in plain English, the stuff you do or can do to make your website rank higher when various terms are entered into a search engine. That being said, there are very few people who truly understand how the process works. In my opinion, for every 250 people that say they really get it, only one actually does.

The reason that I bring this up is because it is really easy to fall in love with the sales pitch these people will throw at you. You will hear things like "It takes time to see results," and other variants of how what they are going to do for you is worth the fat price tag that comes with it.

MILLION DOLLAR LESSON: Google is smarter than you and anyone you can hire to make your website rank high. Most SEO companies aren't going to do anything for you that you can't do yourself.

What I just stated is a strong lesson, one that can keep money in your pocket. However, if you aren't willing to do the work, then hiring a reputable company or individual might be warranted. But before you do, take a few minutes and let me tell you what I know.

Search engines are machines and therefore operate with logic. The basic parts of that logic are actually really simple. Larry Page and Sergey Bryn, the two guys who invented Google, met as Ph.D. students at Stanford. In the process of creating Google, they needed a way to determine some kind of ranking. Obviously having words relative to the search terms was a requirement, but after that, they needed a way to determine what order the results appeared in. Based on their own background, and all of the papers and scientific publications they had either written or read, they felt that the number of citations (or *links*) a site had directed at it should be a major factor in determining which results ranked higher. That being said, some data sources were more credible than others, so they took that into account when they created their search engine algorithm. Meaning, websites that had a whole lot of links directed at them were probably being "cited" or "referenced" because they had more "street cred" than others. When those websites in turn linked to others, that link had more weight than ones from other sites. If you want to go one step deeper, they even looked at what the link itself said. For example, you see a link on a page and it says "Million Dollar Bedroom." That link is worth a lot to the page it is linked to when those same words are entered into a search box and the page shows up in the results.

Now that you have a little background on the basics of how Google originally worked, I need to break your heart. Google now has *hundreds* of factors that determine how your searches are found. And they sure aren't telling anyone how many, what they do, or which ones are more important than others. Why? Because if they did, then it would make it really easy to "game the system" as they like to say. This is also the reason why your "SEO Guy" probably doesn't, in fact, have a bag of magic beans.

"Wait! I like magic beans, and I want some!" Me too, but I regret to inform you that any "magic beans" that make you #1 in Google searches are located right next to the unicorn farm. But they *did* once exist. Many, many years ago there were in fact a lot of tricks and secrets that you could use to push you to the top. But as part of Google's evolution, it now just penalizes you for trying. Hang out for a bit and I will tell you how gut-wrenching that feeling is, then roll right into explaining how screwed you are after getting penalized.

Basic SEO Practices You Can Do That Matter

I scared you on purpose because you need to take this stuff seriously. Engaging in the wrong activity or contracting the wrong people can do irreparable damage to your online presence. Accept that you are about to run a marathon, not a short sprint. And anything that offers shortcuts around that is risky. These tactics are referred to as "Black Hat SEO." Yes, I have tried many of these things thinking I could outsmart "The Man." Nope.

My first recommendation is to start researching "White Hat SEO." These are the things that are considered to be above board. Many are more or less approved by Google. I really don't even like saying that, though, because their standards change so frequently.

If you're looking for advice or suggestions about SEO, skip any article, book, blog or anything else that wasn't written very recently. I mean *within a few months recently*. Why? Because the rules change A LOT. Old articles might be telling you what was great two years ago, and their tips may in fact have worked well. If so, people probably abused it thoroughly, which then meant Google probably changed the rules. Got it?

Next tip. Have you noticed that I'm only talking about Google? Well, there is a reason. It's because Google usually has two-thirds of all the action. Yes, that is correct—approximately two out of every three searches occur on Google. Some of Google's competitors now just license Google search, so if you win on Google, you win other places too. Focus your efforts on Google and be happy if you accidentally get results on the other search engines.

Now, let's examine the most basic stuff. If you are running or starting a business that has a physical location, then you need to register for Google Maps. If done properly, this alone can drive significant business. If you haven't already done this crucial step, put the book down and come back after you list your business. Why the rush? Because they don't put you on the map right away. In order to guarantee that you are who you say you are, they will mail you a postcard with a verification code. No code, no listing. It takes 1–3 weeks to arrive too, so go now! I'll be waiting.

Did you register, or had you already? Great! Now complete your ENTIRE listing. I mean anything and everything. Google Maps does not like incomplete listings, and why would they? The point is to give *quality* search results. Upload pictures where they let you. Take your phone and record a video to upload too. Fill out descriptions and so on. All of this data is what triggers your results.

We aren't done yet. Google likes it when you use their other products and then, in turn, use those products with each other. For instance, Google owns YouTube, so if you have a YouTube video of your business or whatever, then connect that to your Google Maps listing. When you're done, make a Google Plus page for your business and then connect it.

Now let's talk about your website. Do you have one? If you don't, you need one. I really don't care to hear any excuse about why it doesn't exist. I see too many businesses make this rookie mistake. They think they either don't need one or find some way to justify just using a Facebook page. Let me ask you a question. As a consumer, do you most likely find or select a business with a website or without? Enough said.

If you don't have a website yet, you can have one online and ready within a few hours. Our modern world is awesome like that. You don't even need a website designer or developer, or to be a "Tech Person" yourself. You just need about twenty dollars a month and some time. Sites like Wix.com and SquareSpace more or less have fill-in-the-blank type processes for getting you online quick. Most likely you will pay a small subscription, but some don't even ask for one (though you might have to deal with unwanted ads or something like that). Don't be cheap with your site. It is the modern day business card. Take a little time and set up one of the many polished templates offered through these services. If you don't find it user-friendly or you dislike it, move on! Try a competitor. Overall, it is so easy that you are likely to be mad you didn't do it sooner.

As for your site itself, don't overthink it. Make sure to present the most basic and fundamental information about your business in a place where it is easily seen. Don't make people search for your contact information. Avoid using weird fonts and obnoxious colors. The test I like to run is as follows. Pull up your website then turn off your monitor. Ready? Turn it back on, count to three, and then turn it off again. In those few seconds of viewing, were you able to clearly find and understand the following:

What does the business do?

How can they contact you?

If not, you need to go back to the drawing board.

Ten years ago, websites used to have pages that were loaded with all kinds of text and content. This is no longer the case. Often times for the reasons I just mentioned. I now refer to the modern Internet as a "Picture Book," which I feel is totally appropriate.

People have neither the attention span nor interest in reading overly verbose descriptions and reasons why you are awesome. I'm sure it's a great story, much like the one I am telling here, but the reality is that you are better off making information bold and succinct. If possible, use icons or images that clearly show, define, or detail what you do or the message you are trying to communicate. Half of your visitors are going to be on a mobile device. Do you remember the last time you used your phone to visit a site or app? Ever had those moments when you are rapidly sliding your finger up or down while everything on the screen flies by? *That* is how long you have to deliver your message.

There's one more really important thing about your website and the basic SEO associated with it. Critical elements aren't shown on the visible page. I refer to this as "off-page SEO." In technical terms, this involves the **page source**, which you can view on any page using Google Chrome. Just right-click and then select "Page Source" from the options. A new tab will open and you will then see all of the coding associated with the page. No, you don't need to learn how to read all that; however, there are few parts that are crucial.

Located within all of the coding and lines of stuff are the **page title** and **page description**—two big things that you absolutely cannot ignore.

Page title is exactly what it sounds like—a short label of what is on that page. This is where you should accurately and strategically describe what the page is about. If you are a lawn service in Kansas City, your page title might be "Kansas City Lawn and Landscaping Services." Places where you see page titles and probably don't even know it are in the website links that the search engine returns and in the text that shows on the tabs in your web browser. Make your page title 5–7 words. Don't get greedy and make it really long.

The next part of your page that really matters is your page description. Once again, this is exactly what it sounds like—it's a description of your page. Using the same example from above, the page description might say, "Providing lawn care and maintenance for homes in and around the Kansas City area. We mow, mulch, remove leaves, maintain sprinklers, and also do landscaping." The recommended length for a page description is 155 characters. Please note that I said CHARACTERS, not words. As long as you are in that range, you probably aren't upsetting any search engines.

Since you made it through all of this exciting SEO talk, you now get a prize! If you have the ability to control the words in your URL, then you are really in great shape. By this, I don't mean your .com or whatever suffix. I am referring to what comes *after* your suffix.

For example:

.com/kansas-city-lawn-care

A beautifully balanced mix of these three components and a small amount of content on your page—containing words related to what you want to be found for—is often all you need. And by the way, having some keywords that you want to be found for in your domain name isn't a bad idea either.

In conclusion, you need to think like a search engine. By this, I mean logically. If you don't have any of the words you want to be found for listed in any of these areas, why would you expect Google to find you? Follow this basic logic and you will automatically be ahead of those who don't understand these things.

The Long Tail

I like selling stuff. You should too if you want to make a lot of money. So let me bring you up to speed on how to make sales FAST if you are just getting started. When you are selling things online, you have several avenues that you can pursue. In fact, we already talked about one grassroots solution when I discussed posting free ads online via Craigslist. Now I want to get you acquainted with the concept of the "long tail."

First, I want you to picture a basic graph—the kind with the good old X- and Y-axis. On the left side of this graph, it measures really high, then as it moves to the right, it quickly descends down to what, if measured in single units, is barely above zero, but definitely still there. Now picture this going on for a mile. This is the long tail!

Now back to the tall left side—this is your stuff that is the most popular. If we were talking about music, this would be Taylor Swift or Jay-Z or whoever else is hot right now. That being said, this is also where the most competition exists. If you are just getting into whatever it is that you are doing, or perhaps in a space where some big box competitors exist, then just assume that you can't play there. However, what you *can* do with less effort and expense, while most likely getting faster results too, is to start taking bites out of that long tail. Why? Because there isn't much competition there. That doesn't mean it's not worth it, though. In fact, I can tell you that I have made a whole lot of money working the long tail. A popular phrase that comes to mind is "It's hard to go broke taking profits."

Remember how earlier I was unable to offer a blueprint on SEO because things keep changing? Well, it's NOT true in this case. You can easily publish blog articles, online ads, and create pages on your website that, if focused, will most likely make you smile before you frown. The only catch is that you have to do a whole lot of them to make a difference because the long tail is inherently less popular. Think of this like you would fishing. The more lines you have in the water, the more fish you might catch.

A Mad Scientist Is Born

Long before the bedroom office, and even before moving into the house, I had fortunately gained a lot of insight about sales and marketing. I managed to get the whole process of figuring out what is good and what isn't down to three words. Ready?

Test, Test, Test!

Yes, that's it. You just don't really know what will work until you try it.

43

If you are wondering what tests or trials brought me to the beautifully simple concept of long tail marketing, then allow me to share more of my tale. I'm hoping to drive traffic to a website that sells event tickets. So I'm comparing search engine terms like "Justin Bieber tickets" versus "Justin Bieber Indianapolis tickets" and countless other combinations. Somewhere between what felt like ten million and twenty-seven million searches, the fog lifted and I saw the pattern. I should point out that Jill, who is now my wife, compared me to the crazy person Russell Crowe portrays in *A Beautiful Mind*, and rightfully so, as I had become completely obsessed with "cracking the code" of online marketing. In addition to acting like a crazy person, I was starting to look like Tom Hanks in *Castaway*. And I don't mean the part before he is trapped on the island for four years.

For these longer, more specific searches, the exact same sites kept coming up at the top of the search. YES! There *is* a pattern! So I set out to reverse engineer what these people were doing to get this regular placement. I quickly figured out that the two sites that seemed to always be on top were somehow able to create unique webpages—and a large volume of them—almost immediately after new events were announced. I also noticed that their URLs had really specific keywords in them. Not long after, I discovered that the page title and page descriptions had specific patterns too. So how on earth were they doing this? At this point in our web development timeline, when we wanted to add a new page for a newly announced event, we literally had to request that our local web guy add it. I knew there had to be a better way.

What I did know was that all of the information on my website came from an extremely large file that TicketNetwork updated every couple of hours. By large, I mean the equivalent of an Excel spreadsheet that has twenty-six columns and ninety thousand rows. That's a lot of data. In 2009, with bandwidth what it was and processors much slower than now, just the act of downloading this file took a few minutes. Somehow my competitor was taking this data and using it to create pages in a rapid-fire way. Overall, their pages looked like crap, but who cares! They were clearly doing something right.

Possessing this tiny bit of knowledge, I requested a meeting with our web developer. (I have yet to mention I was paying him forty dollars an hour. At the time, that was A LOT.) I realized that if I could somehow duplicate this process, it could be BIG! With the meeting scheduled for the following day, I buried my head in a notebook, trying to do the best I could to describe the recent discovery. Now feels like an appropriate time to tell you that I am a world-renowned stick figure artist. I don't limit this ability to just stick people either. I break it out when drawing up web sketches or concepts. Okay, real talk—I am actually the world's *worst* artist. I can't even draw a stick figure. Despite this, I managed to sketch out what I believed the process might involve.

The next day at the meeting, I laid out my plan. What? This might actually work? Sweet, let's try! What I had mapped out was a method of taking large amounts of data, then using the different variables to create a process that shuffled these variables onto unique webpages, while at the same time not duplicating the page or the content from one page to the next. Does that sound easy or not? I was determined to give it a try.

So we started the development process and it seemed to go well at first. Fast forward two months. We were lost in Stuck City! And I'm losing a lot of confidence and money too. My local developer had made some progress, however he just couldn't get it to go past the third or fourth page before it would more or less go haywire and just make an unlimited supply of the same page. Why was it doing that? If I knew, I wouldn't be here in Stuck City.

Another frustrating month passes, with another three thousand dollars. Is this really this hard? At this point, the local developer was telling me that we would need someone proficient in the programming language known as PHP. Well guess what? In 2009, that wasn't a skill that many US programmers had in their toolbox. Why? Well, as it turns out, we (meaning educators in the United States) taught everyone HTML while growing up. At the time, that was more or less a "static" thing. Meaning, it wasn't conducive to changing pages, but also it didn't really seem to agree with this automatic process I wanted to create. Looks like I was going to need to be the hunter here, not the hunted.

It took me about an hour to figure out that while young aspiring computer programmers in North

America were learning HTML, that wasn't the case in a lot of other countries. Knowing that the payoff could be relatively big, I rolled up my sleeves and got ready to figure out what I needed to do to make this happen.

MILLION DOLLAR LESSON: The harder it is to do something, the less people will be doing it. The same goes with expense. The more expensive an endeavor, the less people will try it. This is called "barrier to entry." Things with a high barrier can also have a BIG payoff. That doesn't mean that something difficult to do will *always* be profitable if you figure it out. However, when it comes to entrepreneurism, this is often the setup for what becomes a story about making a bunch of money.

A Conversation with
Jaysse Lopez of Urban Necessities

Have you ever heard the term "sneakerhead"? It's a real thing, I promise. Well, Jaysse Lopez, owner of Urban Necessities in Las Vegas, is rapidly becoming one of the Internet's most popular and well-known sneakerheads.

Most don't know the extent of the sneaker market. It racks up over fifty-five billion dollars in sales worldwide and also has a robust secondary market orbiting it. By secondary, I mean resale, and it is estimated that the secondary sneaker market eclipsed one billion dollars in total sales volume a while ago. Those Air Jordans that you woke up so early to try and buy online, or perhaps waited in line for and never got, are often sold to willing buyers through various secondary channels.

So what does this have to do with the Million Dollar Bedroom? A lot actually. Jaysse and his wife, Joanie, have a story similar to mine. They too started their business in a somewhat accidental manner—at what may have been one of the worst times in their lives to do so—and then built a really amazing business in the following years. So let's get into it.

MATT: When did you open your retail store in Vegas?

48

JAYSEE: We opened the store on September 17, 2014.

Tell me about what led to you opening the store.

In the months before that, I had gone through a tough time to say the least…I got laid off from my job, evicted from my apartment, and my car got repo'd. I also met Joanie, who as you know is now my wife. Now I've always loved sneakers, and there was a sneaker coming out that I wanted to buy, but I didn't have the funds for it. So I knew I had to get creative. I looked into possibly buying shoes to sell them, so I could get this shoe for free. The shoe came out. Joanie added to the cash that I managed to put together, and I was able to buy nineteen pairs. I sold eighteen, kept a pair for myself, and made a $200 profit on each sale. That was the first sneaker we bought.

Over the next few months, I did that again and again.

Three months later, we opened the website.

After 6–7 months, Joanie and I split, and then I switched the business to consignment because I couldn't really move around (as I didn't have a car). There was a sneaker event coming. I was down to my last couple pairs of shoes and was planning to go to the event just to sell them and then buy a plane ticket to go back home. And in the process of getting some other shoes together for consignment, it turned into 600+ pairs within a month. And, at that point, I realized that if I could get that many shoes on pretty much spit handshakes, then a store might be possible.

Two months before the store opened, I went from *maybe I'll open a store* to *I'm going to open a store*. By then back together with Joanie, we willed it into existence. When I signed the lease for the mall space, I had forty dollars to my name. It was hard pitching our dream of something bigger to someone when you couldn't really communicate it on paper.

Did you do anything else to prepare in the two months prior to opening?

At that time, I did a lot of market research, visiting other stores. I saw opportunity in other people's problems.

Such as?

There is too much paperwork and other work in the consignment process. No one was willing to do the dirty work. I'm a big sports fan, and I know that everyone wants to be a superstar, but you need a team. I mean, everyone remembers Michael Jordan, but what about the BJ Armstrongs of the world? The Bulls weren't going to win all of the titles without the TEAM. At the end of the day, we're not all going to be superstars. It was a tough message to pitch, but the core team bought in.

Whenever you open a new business, you are forced to learn a lot of new stuff FAST. What did you have to learn?

Taxes, the entire credit card process, and then legal stuff. With taxes, good old Uncle Sam wants his, and regularly. Learning how to get that right was a lot. Then with the credit card stuff, we took some shortcuts in the beginning and left ourselves exposed, then got burned a few times. Then the legal stuff; there's a lot of it. Takes a while to *get it*.

What is the most important lesson that you have learned about opening a business?

You have to sacrifice any sort of time that you think you have. Be open to doing what the next guy isn't going to do. You have to have a foundation to grow. You don't start building the high rise from the 30th floor and then work your way down.

If you could give the "old you" advice now, what would it be?

Be careful who you hire. Not everybody is going to work as hard as you. That can happen, however, some people are just going to jump on for the ride. It's probably best to let your friends and family stay exactly that.

You have built one of the most impressive social media followings I've seen on Instagram. Tell me more about that. (On December

31, 2016 they had 168k followers; on January 24, 2017, the date of this interview, it was already up to 184k.)

It was at 25k followers going into 2016, and I told my staff that the goal was 150k by end of the year. We beat it at 168k. New goal by end of 2017 is to reach 400k.

What do you think the biggest factors for social media growth are?

A few things. Number one is consistency. If you look at our Instagram feed, we take advantage of it as basically free advertising. Some days we post 30–70 times/day. No one wants to post and reply to comments and messages 12–15 hours/day, but I'd do it 24 hours a day if I could.

People don't see the hidden benefit of posting the same thing over and over again. It comes back to building the ground floor to build the high rise. If you do it enough, sooner or later it sticks and everyone starts paying attention.

The other reason is that as the brand is grown organically—and through good business practices—you start attracting a different type of customer. As customers are coming in and buying, and as they're moving more and more volume, consigners hear how good their turnaround time is, which gets better products and, in turn, better customers, and it keeps growing.

Also, I'm at the store every day personally thanking each customer who comes in, trying to find out how they heard about the shop and what they think. It's going above and beyond that's worked.

What role do you think your social media following and its massive growth has played in the growth of sales at the store and the website?

I wouldn't even be able to put a price on it. It's our lifeline.

So I've noticed at the store that A LOT of people want their picture taken with you. How does that feel?

It's surreal. Sometimes I think, "You want your picture taken with me?" At the end of the day, every one of those people are not obligated to pay attention, much less spend their dollars or come down to the shop. I'm just happy they do that. Taking a picture with any of them is the least I can do.

I've noticed they want your autograph, too!

Yeah, I'm still getting used to that part. In fact, I'm not good at it. One time I had this kid ask me to sign the shoes he just bought. I did a terrible job—so bad that I bought him a new pair after and then got it right.

Overall, it's the same as the pictures. I can't believe that you would want my autograph. It's still mind-blowing. I don't want to forget where I'm from. I don't want to forget my struggle because that becomes my fear. I don't want to go back to that. But I remember that guy and I'm like "Would you ask *that* guy for an autograph?" It's still kind of crazy. Sometimes I still get the shakes when people ask for my autograph. It's weird.

Don't feel too bad. There are a few copies of my first book in the trash can for similar reasons.

*** A few months after this conversation, Jaysse, Joanie Lopez, and I became business partners in the newly formed 2 J's Kicks LLC, an online marketing company based around Jaysse's expertise and growing outreach in the sneaker business. Stay tuned as we plan on doing nothing less than offering our best.

SECTION TWO:

IT'S ALWAYS SUNNY IN CEBU CITY

AT KELLEY SCHOOL OF BUSINESS, I heard the terms "outsource" and "offshore" about ten thousand times each. These terms were still relatively fresh for a lot of business people, including myself, in 2009. Just in case you aren't familiar, to offshore a job is to hire someone from a country other than your own. This is done to create a more favorable expense structure for your business. Just because you are paying less for a job doesn't necessarily mean it's unfair. If you have ever traveled to foreign countries, you may have noticed that the almighty dollar may in fact go a little further elsewhere.

However, while I was hearing these terms a lot, what I wasn't hearing was how you go about finding this help. Did I need to jump on the next flight to India, China, or somewhere else? How does this work?

MILLION DOLLAR LESSON: Google will help you find the answer to just about anything. You just have to keep digging until you figure it out.

Armed with nothing more than a strong desire to get the most for my money, I started researching. I found that several countries had a fairly strong pool of affordable workers ready to help. Hmm…that doesn't really narrow it down. So I dug deeper. India and China came to mind, and then a little further research suggested the Philippines. Fair enough. Let's see what's out there.

I quickly found a lot of information about the outsource industry associated with each country. There were definitely a lot more factors to consider than I'd imagined, such as:

- Time zone differences
- Language barriers
- Each country's different areas of expertise (I'll explain soon)
- Geopolitical issues (Also coming soon)
- Infrastructure considerations
- Currency exchange rates

At first I hadn't really considered how the time zone difference would possibly impact everything. Once you give it some thought, it's really obvious, but for the most part, people don't want to become nocturnal in order to do their jobs. Also, several countries don't have daylight savings time.

In regards to language barriers or differences, I have always found it amusing that Americans, who usually speak only one language fluently, often expect the rest of the world to also speak this language. Since I am one of these people, I was definitely going to need to find help that spoke English. Ugh, this was getting complicated.

Then I started reading about how certain countries trend toward certain skills. At that point, I was not very versed with technology, meaning I'm not a programmer.

What's the difference between PHP and HTML? What's a database? That's just an Excel file, right?

I was starting to feel like I was in over my head.

On top of everything, I had to consider geopolitical issues AND infrastructure stuff too? Not everyone worldwide has Internet and electricity all day every day. Not everyone lives in a neighborhood unconcerned that some form of social or political unrest is about to break out at any moment. And wait, how would I pay these workers? Would it be in US dollars? How was I actually going to get the money to them? In fact, how was I even going to know that they were working?

At this point, I considered simply hiring local.

But after taking a few days to continue my research, I had an epiphany. The cleaning service my parents have used for fifteen years is owned by a man from the Philippines. He's also one of the nicest people I know. Maybe he has some insight. So I gave him a call. At first I did feel a little hesitant, after all I was asking how I can go about hiring his fellow countrymen and countrywomen for cheaper than I would pay locals. What happened next surprised me.

I found someone incredibly proud of where he was from. I could feel the positive energy streaming through the phone as he spoke of how hardworking and honest "his people" were, and how I wouldn't regret hiring "his people." Okay, that made me feel a lot better. Now what? I explained that I needed computer programmers and he informed me that while he was from Manila, Cebu City was considered the technology hub of the

Philippines. Huh. Never heard of it. I thanked him for his time and ended the call feeling really great about the Philippines. Maybe if I didn't find a programmer there, I might at least consider a visit.

As it turned out, Cebu City was in fact considered the hot spot for tech jobs in the country. It's the second largest city too, meaning there should be plenty of people. In addition, the time zone difference was twelve hours. That meant it wouldn't interfere with my classes or ticket business. Cool! Then it got even better. Most people in the Philippines not only spoke English but also observed Christian beliefs. That being said, I'm not religious; however, my research pointed out that knowing and understanding the culture you were doing business with made things easier. It also gave you a level of understanding when it came to holidays and religious dates that you might have in common. By this, I mean Hindus and Muslims don't celebrate Christmas, so while you are having dinner with your family on Christmas Eve and opening presents with your kids on Christmas Day, to them that might just be Wednesday and Thursday. Then later, when something like Ramadan comes around, you might have accidentally set an important deadline in the middle of it, not even knowing that it existed.

Now I needed to advertise this job. This is where things got a little more interesting. In the US, there are lots of sites where posting an employment ad is easy. But that's not the case in Cebu. So after some confusion, I settled on placing an ad in the online version of the

Cebu City newspaper. Why not? Wait a minute, a Philippine *Peso*? Isn't that the currency of Mexico? As it turns out, the Philippines also calls their currency the peso. So many details, but I can handle this. So off we go, posting our first international employment ad.

Wait! How was I going to talk to these candidates? Through email? Something else? This was when I discovered Skype. Fairly new and revolutionary at the time, considering that people still commonly used things like AOL Messenger, this Skype thing said that it would let me not only have text chat, but I could also talk to people *for free* worldwide. Wow. Go technology! So I set up my free account and posted my username and email address in the ad.

Over the next couple of days, the emails trickled in and I engaged in some conversations. Eventually I found a guy that, while still currently employed, seemed like he might be a good fit. I explained to him the problems that I was having with my local guy not being able to get past one certain block when it came to my automatic page creator concept. Having a strong desire to be helpful— and despite still not being paid—he offered to take a look at the code. About an hour later, he sent an email with a short response and what then very much looked like gibberish. There was no way the solution was that easy. Regardless, I sent this over to the local guy. Another couple hours passed and I got a response from my local developer saying nothing more than "IT WORKED!"

Seriously?

I knew I had my guy. Now I needed to figure out how to negotiate a salary and hire someone who was almost exactly on the other side of the planet from me. I called the helpful guy who owns the cleaning service again for advice.

During my second call, I learned that in the Philippines it is often customary for a new employee to go through the equivalent of a trial period. If it was a newly graduated student from one of the local universities, then this was pretty much a certainty. Seemed reasonable enough. Now what do I pay them? Meaning, what's fair? My intention was to get bang for my buck; at the same time, I'm not a monster. It was then shared with me that the US dollar could, in many locations in the Philippines, buy 4–7 times more for the same price as the United States. I specifically remember the example of a bottle of rum, and being told that the ten-dollar bottle here was about two dollars there. So, therefore, if I paid someone a thousand dollars a month, in relative lifestyle, it was worth four thousand and maybe as high as seven thousand a month there. This made me feel better about what I was about to do. So I sent the offer for exactly that—one thousand dollars a month salary. My offer was accepted, but I was going to have to wait a month for him to start. Fair enough. We had a deal.

The Outsource Formula

I'm going to put the cart in front of the horse for a minute and tell you that ever since hiring my first employee in Cebu City in 2009, I have had multiple employees in the city, including present day. The reason I bring this up is because I feel that it's a good time to share my Outsource Formula with you. It's not complex.

For this example, we will use two employees. One makes ten dollars an hour; the other makes fifty. That gives us a one to five ratio. That being said, the fifty an hour worker needs to either do things five times faster or five times better than the one who makes ten in order to maintain an equal output per dollar. There are a few other factors to consider. Your own time MUST be figured into the calculation, so you are going to need to reasonably consider what you are worth per hour. If you find yourself needing to spend time directing, supervising, or instructing either employee, that counts. So if your time is also worth fifty dollars per hour, and it takes you one hour to instruct or supervise the less expensive employee, then they might not be less expensive after all.

MILLION DOLLAR LESSON: The president of the company shouldn't be spending all of his or her time supervising, instructing, and managing the lowest wage employees in the company.

Overall, you can quickly and easily change the landscape and output of your business by using various offshore or outsource workers. But make sure that you always take my formula into consideration. The employees and operations I ended up building in Cebu City became essential to my success. People ask me, "So how often do you have to go over there?" Well, as of 2017, I still have never been to the Philippines—not because I don't want to, but instead because I haven't *had* to go there.

Now off to the races. It took a little while to really get the Automatic Page Creator (which we just called the "APC") running smoothly. However, once smoothed out, we quickly realized that we could create anywhere from two thousand to three thousand pages a minute. Yes, you read that correctly. Our newly invented process could, using nothing more than the equivalent of an Excel spreadsheet, make unique web pages and create unique content for each page that fast.

Keep in mind, what we had just built in 2009 was pretty amazing. To the best of my knowledge, there wasn't more than one other competitor doing it. And as it turns out, we were doing it better because, after a few weeks, we noticed our pages were consistently just above the competitor's.

As our pages climbed in the rankings, so did our sales. However, so did the demands on our resources. And by resources, I mean the phone was ringing all of the time. Now it's important to point out that the "Million Dollar Bedroom" was only about ten feet away from the bedroom where I slept. There was no real retreat from work. Not that I was complaining. In fact, I was remarkably excited with the sheer volume of incoming sales. But the windfall of activity strained our cash flow. All these new sales coming in required us to pay for tickets immediately while waiting for credit card batches to settle. Overall, I like to say, "Sales Cures Ails," so we just kept at it!

You Can't Compete with My Non-Compete

With recent additions to the team we now had three people working together in one small bedroom. So I moved my work stuff into the third bedroom right across the hall. That's right, the Million Dollar Bedroom was now *plural* (as I luckily had two extra bedrooms).

Business was good. The newest programmer had solved our situation, the phone was ringing, the inbox was pinging with incoming sales, and…I was about to have my first potential legal issue.

As our new programmer in Cebu became familiar with what we were doing (plus provided services at one quarter of the cost of the local programmer), we basically didn't need the local guy after a few months. My prior experience in the professional world introduced me to the "non-compete agreement." It's an agreement signed by two parties (often between an employer and employee or contractor) that establishes some guidelines about the type of business one or both parties can engage in after the contract or employment ends. Non-compete agreements are very common with programmers because you need some kind of assurance that they aren't going to take what you just paid them to build, put a different name on it, and then sell it themselves.

My father was an attorney. Growing up, it wasn't uncommon to discuss law or things related to it at the dinner table. While I thought it was really boring at the time, that and all of the extra math homework forced on me actually became useful. (Thanks Dad!) I learned that "good fences make good neighbors" or CYA, which means "Cover Your Ass." Before I started working on a regular basis with the local programmer, I did in fact have the foresight to insist on a signed non-compete agreement.

Here are a few basic guidelines in case you need to create one. In order to be enforced, a non-compete agreement must be fair to both parties, somewhat specific, expire within a reasonable amount of time depending on the employment term, and potentially include what recourse could be taken if violated. These agreements might even include specific competitors they can't contract with for a defined period of time after working for you. LAWS ARE DIFFERENT IN EVERY STATE, SO CHECK YOUR LOCAL LAWS, AS I AM ONLY THE SON OF A LAWYER!

To be more specific, your potential non-compete should specify EXACTLY what they aren't going to compete with after your employment. In my case, it read "ticket resale websites and any processes or software created by myself or my company that (insert name) programmer either created or was allowed access to." It included an expiration date of two years past the contract or term of employment ending for any reason—meaning, whether he quit, got fired, or we just didn't have enough work to continue. In conclusion, he wasn't allowed to work for or sell to other companies whose primary function was selling event tickets.

Things your non-compete definitely *shouldn't* contain are overly broad statements like "can't work for a web development company," "never expires," or huge unreasonable remedies if violated. If agreements like this end up in front of a judge, you won't stand a chance. You might be thinking, "But isn't this a contract?" Yes, in nature it is; however, most reasonable judges aren't going to fully allow you to restrict someone else from making a living if they aren't *directly* interfering with your business by doing so. That is why broad, general statements are more or less meaningless. In fact, in some cases, a judge won't even care about your non-compete. You are best checking with an actual attorney before relying too heavily on your non-compete.

Now let me explain its relevance to my situation. I'm sitting at my desk early one afternoon and the phone rang. It was another ticket reseller calling because he noticed my logo on my local developer's website. The two had already spoken and he wanted to know how my experience was working with the developer. Seriously? What happened next shocked me. Not only had the local developer offered to build him a ticket resale site, but he also offered to build him one that performed the EXACT same processes and functions that I had worked so hard to create, and that I'd spent a heck of a lot of money on. Are you KIDDING me? After picking my jaw up off the floor, and taking about six thousand deep breaths, I politely explained to my competitor that there was a non-compete agreement in place and asked if I could make a couple calls and then call him back. After hanging up the phone, and then spewing a remarkably impressive string of obscenities, I calmed down.

MILLION DOLLAR LESSON: Even if you are remarkably pissed off, and feel cheated or wronged, when you address it with the other party, it is imperative to remain calm and professional. It is possible that you don't have the whole story. In addition, calling and immediately laying into someone isn't likely to do much other than make them either hang up on you or just start yelling back.

Now it was time to make the call. Before I dialed the local developer, I made sure to review the entire content of the signed agreement. I even kept it in front of me just in case I needed to reference it.

On the call, I made sure to mention that I had spoken to his potential new client. I then reminded him about our agreement and that what he was doing was very much a direct violation of this agreement.

"All you did was take my code and give it to the guy in Cebu City," he said.

"*Your* code?" I replied, dumbfounded. "Don't you mean *my* code—meaning the code I paid you to write for ME?" Did this guy really think he not only owned this process but also had the rights to sell it? So after reminding him again about our agreement, I ended the call.

A few hours later, still not really sure what to do, I got an email from the local developer. He explained that he didn't want to tell me about this potential client because he was sure that I was going to react the way I did. I want you to now form a mental picture of me planting my face in my palm while shaking my head. OF COURSE I am going to "act this way," and no, I don't want you creating competition for me with my own invention while also collecting revenue from it.

It was time to escalate this just a bit.

When you have an attorney in the family, it means free legal advice, right? Tell them I told you to say that when you ask. In my case it was true, so I made a call to dear old Dad. These calls were always and continue to this day to be funny. I'm pretty sure that my dad hasn't given me any legal insight that didn't include some kind of disclaimer, but the information has always been useful. In this particular case—after he established that as an attorney in Kansas he wasn't 100 percent sure what the laws were in Indiana—he commended me on having enough forward thinking to create the non-compete agreement. Knowing me all too well, he told me to put down the pitchfork and to take another six thousand deep breaths. After refusing to do so for about two minutes, I gave in and listened. Next, he advised me to send a "Cease and Desist Letter." That would create a timestamp of sorts and officially inform the other party of my position and my desire for him to, well, cease and desist these actions. In addition, I was advised to inform the recipient that I felt these actions needed to stop immediately and not doing so would result in me seeking financial damages. The final advice was to make sure to send it with some kind of signature required or proof of delivery. That way, the recipient can't say that they didn't receive it. So that is exactly what I did.

After sending the letter, I called the guy who wanted to hire the local developer. I explained the situation and he understood my position. We actually became colleagues and I ended up selling him the same services that he had requested from the local developer, who, by the way, did very much cease and desist his actions. All in all, a calm, well-thought-out plan and reaction paid off.

TIME FOR THE BUYOUT

As previously mentioned, I had a partner during all of this time. Maybe you noticed there wasn't much said past that. Please remember when I took on a partner I needed the money, not necessarily the help. That sure changed quickly. We were creating sales. We had built an impressive new automated process for building websites. We even had an intern! Despite all of the success, I wasn't feeling fully satisfied. Honestly, I was becoming a little resentful. I resented that I was working sixteen hours a day and my partner wasn't helping much other than financially. That isn't an exaggeration either. I started passing on Tuesday night poker. I stopped doing stuff with my friends. All in all, I wasn't doing much other than obsessively working.

Something had to change, and I knew the only way that I was going to be happy was if I owned 100 percent of my own company again. So I let my partner know that I was interested in buying him out. But he didn't want to sell. Knowing full and well that was his right, I considered my options.

It came down to three: I could just live with it, I could figure out a way to push the buyout (because, after all, there was SOME price that would work), or I could quit. That's right, you read that correctly. I could literally cash out and quit. The online marketing skills that I had uncovered were versatile, and I knew that I wasn't stuck just doing ticket stuff. I *liked* doing it, however, because after years of working around music and having a passion for it, I found it interesting. Let me take a minute and squeeze in another lesson here.

MILLION DOLLAR LESSON: Try to keep your business around things you find interesting. That is what gets you through the days and times where it feels like a grind. The side lesson is that most of us find money interesting, so making a lot of money doing most things will also seem interesting. Or interesting enough.

And we're back. Now I needed to figure out which of these options was going to work. I knew I wasn't happy. I even felt guilty for *not* being happy because, from the age of five, I always knew I was meant to be a business owner. I achieved that dream, so why wasn't I happy? I think in the end most of it came down to not feeling in control. There were other factors involved, but I really just wanted to be the only driver. So before doing anything, I sat down and did a "Pros and Cons" exercise. If you aren't familiar with this, it is where you take a piece of paper, draw a line down the middle, and on the left side list the pros (or the good stuff) and then on the right side the cons (or bad stuff). Seeing the facts side-by-side helps make qualified decisions.

If I chose to just live with the situation:

PROS – I wouldn't have to deal with a buyout; I would keep more money in the company, as a buyout would drain a lot of my cash.

CONS – Continuing displeasure; I would have to keep paying money out to a partner; I was likely to become even unhappier.

If I chose to aggressively seek a buyout:

PROS – Regain control of the company; I would feel in control again; I wouldn't have to feel like I had to create new business entities if I wanted to do stuff not related to the current business.

CONS – Financial strain and dealing with a buyout.

If I chose to just quit:

PROS – Not much except the ability to be free of the arrangement.

CONS – Having to start over; I wouldn't be able to continue with ticket stuff as my partner and I had our own non-compete with each other; I would forever feel like a quitter.

The thing I really like about this exercise is that it puts it all in front of you. Can you immediately see which decision was probably the best? If not, look again. It was the option of getting more aggressive about my buyout—which is exactly what I did.

Having experience and skill in selling will, in my opinion, help you more than anything else when it comes to your own business. Why? Because whether you realize it or not, you are constantly in the act of selling. You are selling ideas, products, opinions, and choices daily. Think about that while I finish this tale.

It was time to buy my company back. Having my initial offer met with a NO, I knew I needed to do better. The desired result was probably going to be expensive, but sometimes that's just the way things go. To boost my chances, I knew I needed a little bit of extra enticement.

I offered a gradual buyout. The buyout gave me instant 100 percent control of the company, but the shares themselves transferred over eighteen months, during which I offered a monthly payment to my partner. These payments were in equal amounts and, unless I defaulted on my payments, I would eventually own 100 percent of the company. The other option I presented was "I quit." I had thought more and more about it too, and at that point, I was very much ready to do so. We were finding success, but I wasn't even making the same amount of money I made before I quit my last job. Now, before I tell you which option my partner chose, I do need to say that my buyout offer was very generous. All in all, he would do quite well considering that the original intention was never to have much more than a short-term venture.

He accepted the offer! I ended up making all of the payments, and, to this day, I still own 100 percent of that same business. While I regained control of my company, it did come at a cost. The monthly buyout payment in many ways gave me the equivalent of a reasonably paid employee who never came to work, but so did my payments pre-buyout. I should also say, since he will probably read this book, my former partner and I are still friends. I wouldn't be able to tell this story if he and I hadn't gotten this whole thing started the way we did. What it came down to was simply my personal and professional happiness. He respected and understood my need for that, then also got paid well for accepting it. All in all, if you get into a deal that you find yourself not happy with later, try and resolve things the right way. It's a lot easier in the end.

The Second Jill

As I mentioned, I have been married twice, both times to women named Jill. Which, by the way, is really confusing later when friends who haven't seen you in ten years come to visit. Anyway, about seven months into the business we started dating. Since this book isn't a love story but instead a story about the love of building a business in my extra bedrooms, I'll get back on track.

Why is this relevant? Because I hired her. Yes, we ended up getting married; however, I don't recommend that you hire your girlfriend to work for your business. In fact, most won't suggest hiring your wife to work for your business either. Why? For the same reasons that you shouldn't hire your friends or family. It can put a strain on the relationship.

Jill and I are truly an example of a successful husband and wife team. But we're an exception. There are important reasons for NOT taking this route. Your spouse may not share the same passion or enthusiasm you have for your business. And when you both work for your business, well, you have all of your eggs in the same basket. This is something you might need to figure out on your own. Just consider what I am saying.

Hiring Jill meant that we now had four people in the house all working for the company. At this point, I set Jill up in the living room. *Here you go. This coffee table is your desk; this couch is your chair.* I should also mention that we had finally made it to 2010! Jill had just graduated from the same school I was attending with a different major, and needed a job. What did I put her in charge of? Learning how to blog. Today the blogosphere—as some now call it—is remarkably accessible, but back then it was still growing its roots.

After a small learning curve, some trial and error research, and a few curse words, we figured out what we needed to do as blog marketers. We added a blog extension to the back of BroadRippleTickets.com, and Jill started plugging away at creating articles about upcoming concert tours and events. We learned a few things really quickly. The first being that deciding on and creating content, a decent layout, and an image couldn't be done quickly. However, we also realized that these articles showed up in Google search sometimes within a few minutes! How was that even possible? Well, during that time, Google was really putting an emphasis on newly created content. They believed that the ability to bring their users the newest, freshest content was essential. This also explained why our page creator program threw pages up so high on the search rankings. It's because it was new, fresh, and FIRST!

I hope that you are noticing that we are getting better at what we do at this point. So let's pause for another quick lesson.

MILLION DOLLAR LESSON: Even if you are already the best at what you do, ALWAYS focus on getting better. Your competition is never that far behind you.

We were really starting to *get it*. And Jill proved to be excellent at this stuff. She created a system where she could use a template for the layout and then mark the areas where certain variables would need to change. And where did that idea originate? It came from our very own page creator program. We started noticing that our blog articles and our own pages for these events often came up number one and number two in searches. The only downside of all this was that we weren't able to create a similar article-generation program for the blogs, which left us still constrained by how many of these things we could publish. But first, another more important issue was getting out of control—our ability to handle all of the incoming sales!

MILLION DOLLAR LESSON: Having too many sales is a blessing not a curse! Figure out how to handle it. Don't EVER do anything to reduce your sales.

In July of 2010, I decided to count how many phone calls we got in a month. I was able to do this by downloading the call records from our phone provider, Vonage. We received over two thousand phone calls the prior month. Wow! Based on sales, that couldn't be right. Let's do some math. If you are "open" five days a week most months, that comes out to about one hundred calls a day. So what's the problem? Well, most of these calls weren't people BUYING stuff; they were calling to ask questions ABOUT buying. We also got a lot of calls that went like this: "I was just calling to see if you guys were real." Then they would hang up and buy something online. It got to the point where callers were on the line for twenty minutes. They had questions like, "How much closer is row B than row C?" It was really taking up A LOT of time, and it was also relatively expensive to pay my staff to take these calls because most didn't result in a sale.

Time to Partner Up

Wait, you're thinking, *I thought you just bought your partner out?* I did. What I'm about to show is how you can often times improve your existing business model by partnering with other companies. These win-win situations are incredibly common and profitable if done well.

Was our model sustainable? Was I headed toward running some weird call center in my home? Hold up. I already *was* running a weird call center in my home! So I decided to see what my options were. I called TicketNetwork. After all, it was their technology being used as the backbone for the operation. This is when I had my first "You mean I could have been doing that all along?" moment. My rep explained to me that they had what they called a "Partner Program." How did it work? Well, they handled the calls and nearly everything else. All our website would become was a marketplace. By that, I mean everything just passed through our site. We didn't have to collect the money (saving the roughly 3 percent per transaction for credit card processing); it just passed through to the seller. We kept the service fees and TicketNetwork kept its 2 percent of the sales volume. We also didn't have to deal with fulfilling the order—that was up to the seller to accept or reject. Most importantly, we didn't have to deal with all of the calls.

I decided to take a little time to think about it. The next day, we received around two hundred calls and my decision was made. Well mostly. I had one more issue. How would they even know the caller was calling from my site? The rep told me that their reps asked each caller which site they visited. Eh…I didn't like that iffy confirmation at all. Fortunately, we had built things up to doing a volume of sales that impressed them enough to give us our very own new phone number there. Problem solved.

As we prepared to make this switch, we realized that we still had a couple of things to clean up. The first being that our existing phone number was posted and published in A LOT of places. Annoying and time consuming, but still manageable to fix. Then we had our old number on a whole lot of webpages on our own site—nearly 100,000 pages total. NO PROBLEM. Why? While we truly appreciated our automated page creation program for other reasons up to this point, we now realized that we could easily make this change, or other changes in the future, by simply changing our template and then regenerating all of the pages again. Why was this amazing? Think about how long it would take you to make one change on 100,000 different anything.

After the switch, the change was INSTANT. The phone stopped ringing but the sales were still coming in. Amazing!

One of the biggest stress relievers was that by no longer having to process the payments, we simultaneously removed our exposure to fraud liability. Any time you take a credit card payment from anyone, there are a couple things to consider. The first is that the person using the card may not in fact be who they say they are. This is fraud. That being said, the credit card companies hold the merchant responsible. Online credit card fraud was particularly rampant at the time. It was even worse for things that were or could be delivered electronically, like a PDF file that gets printed out and used as your event ticket. By the time the credit card account holder realizes there are unauthorized charges on their card, it is almost always too late for the merchant to do anything. This results in your second possible position of liability: the "chargeback." I sit here and cringe, as this is a dirty, dirty word for business owners. A chargeback is what occurs when a buyer either claims fraudulent use or has some other issue or dispute with whatever product or service you provided.

MILLION DOLLAR LESSON: Learn how to mitigate loss and do so quickly. Enabling business practices that reduce your position of liability should always be a priority. Not doing so can become a really big problem, even a business killer, often before you even know the problem exists.

Because it is so important that you understand this concept, I want to show you a quick and easy example of how *just one* chargeback or fraudulent order can ruin your numbers.

Imagine five sales total. The cost of goods on each is $80. You sold the item for $100. Minus the 3 percent credit card fee, you have $97, minus the $80 unit cost, leaving you with a per-item gross margin of $17. Thus you have $85 ($17 x 5) to pay toward other expenses, hopefully leaving you with a profit. We aren't even going there yet.

Now let's say one of these five sales was fraud or resulted in a chargeback (both are the same in the end for the most part). The credit card company will send you notification that this is occurring as they quickly pull this money back from your account while everything is sorted out. They do so to minimize their own liability. They also charge you around $25 for the pain in the ass "you" are causing them. If you don't have a signature on a credit card receipt, you are going to lose 99 percent of the time. In my case, all of the sales are online, so I don't have a signature. You will be allowed to send a reply, however you are probably screwed, resulting in you never seeing this money again.

Now let's redo our math.

Okay, same five sales, same cost of goods, but now adjusted:

This time we still originally collect $400, but, with the $25 chargeback fee, we're left with only $375. But the cost of goods on five items sold was $80 each or $400 total. Do you see where this is going?

So now not only did we lose the potential profit of what we thought was a sale, but we also negated the potential positive gain on four others. Keep in mind, we haven't even discussed labor or other expenses that might exist.   As you can see, this can get out of control in a hurry. In this example, we used a linear cost of goods. Imagine what it would look like if the fraudulent or contested order was three times larger than the other four! Now you can see why creating a better position of liability is so important.

In conclusion, the entire switch saved us money in just about every single instance we found. The best part though was that without answering the phone and talking to housewives all day about Taylor Swift tickets, we could focus on building even more sales and capitalize on our newfound growth.

MILLION DOLLAR LESSON: On the most basic level, smart business is easy to understand. You either need to *spend less* or *sell more*. But if you are really doing it right, then you find ways to do *both*.

Building an Online Army

With the phone not ringing a hundred times a day, the focus was back on building our empire. At this point, it would have been easy to keep on keeping on, but if you haven't figured it out yet, that really isn't my style. I'm not a "managing" kind of guy. Instead, I'm always looking for ways to expand a business and keep it growing.

Having successfully hired someone in the Philippines, I figured that we could probably find more people interested in creating this win-win arrangement. The problem was that hiring our first guy was a fairly involved process, in that I had to do A LOT of emailing back and forth, trying to chat through Skype. At that time, I felt like I needed to do something FAST, because I knew that my competition most likely wasn't far behind.

MILLION DOLLAR LESSON: In business, success is near-guaranteed to bring others' imitation. Any unique position or approach you create is likely on the clock.

Still a student at this point, I learned that in business you have a few ways to succeed: you could do it better, faster, or cheaper. Without any of these, you don't possess any kind of advantage.

So I consulted Google looking for ways to hire more offshore workers. I immediately came across Upwork (formerly oDesk), an online marketplace where contractors offer services and clients can hire them to perform a service. It gets better. It not only logged a timecard for them, and then paid them the same way you pay anyone else, but it also held the worker accountable for actually doing the work. How? By taking five random screenshots of their desktop each hour. Brilliant! Their software also measured things like mouse clicks and keyboard strokes. Even better!

So I gave it a shot and posted an ad in their marketplace looking for a "Blog Specialist." Well, I got around seventy-five replies to my new ad *in less than twenty-four hours*. It was awesome but overwhelming. Where to begin? First, I went through the profiles for each potential worker, yet wasn't really able to determine much to help set them apart. One thing I *did* notice was that some of these people had already performed services for others and there were reviews. Great! So I used that to thin my pool. To keep it brief, I ended up hiring six people. Go big or go home, right? I hired people from India, China, and, yes, Cebu City. Why is that last part important? Because, at this point, I was already considering what I might need to do if this worked out. If we ever opened a physical office overseas, having people in the same city might be a good idea. The business was barely a year old and already we are talking about opening offices overseas? Yep, that's how fast it can happen.

Now that we had six more people ready to work, we soon learned we weren't quite as prepared as we thought we were. My only experience with outsourcing up until then was our current programmer. But surely these new folks could easily produce blog articles based on Jill's templates, right?

What I found was that explaining this process to others and getting them to duplicate it was a lot harder than I thought it would be. Within a week, I ended the contract with two of the contractors due to the fact that I was having such a hard time communicating through the language barrier. A week later, I cut two more—one of which I found playing video games when he said he was working thanks to the screenshots I was able to see via oDesk's software! The other one just wasn't producing consistent results. By that, I mean he would work for eight hours then wouldn't work at all for a few days. After two weeks, we had only two new contractors left—one of which I was having a hard time reaching, but at the same time was really, really getting the work done! Then a week later, the other person still left quit, not because of anything we did, but because she found something better.

And then there was one. It happened to be a guy from Cebu. I finally established better and more regular communication with him, yet I noticed that he wasn't working the full forty-hour allotment. I asked why. He explained that he actually had another job. Even though mine paid five times more, he was reluctant to quit the other. Finding a job wasn't easy there, and unlike the United States, stuff like unemployment benefits didn't exist. Still curious, I asked more questions. As it turns out, both he and his wife worked at an office that provided data entry services for an American company that I won't name. And they were paid a whopping sixty cents an hour. I thought, *Holy shit, how does anyone even live on that?* I felt guilty for paying them three dollars an hour. He told me that the job I provided was a "blessing" for his family and expressed a desire to do it full-time again.

So I gave him a commitment that I would provide enough tasks that he could work up to fifty hours a week, and then I offered his wife a job too!

Over the next couple of months, this husband and wife team were AMAZING. They were not only reliable and easy to communicate with, but also worked so hard. I might be on to something here.

At this stage, I felt like it might be time to get some of these people in Cebu City together in the same room. I had grown to not only like but also trust the programmer I had hired. Although we had never met in person, I could tell through his dedication and appreciation of the job that he was the kind of person I could work with. I'll give you a quick example. Every time I would send him his pay through PayPal, he sent me a thank you email. I even tried telling him that he didn't need to do that. It was money he earned and, while I really appreciated the work, he wasn't in a spot of needing to thank me. I even told him that I was the one who should be thanking him! Regardless, those emails kept coming, and continue to come because he still works with me.

So the Cebu City meeting was set. Three people I have never met were going to meet up at a local café. After the meeting, my programmer told me that he really liked the other guy and his wife and felt like they were "good people." That was good enough for me at the time.

Since we were selling more and more and getting better at it, I decided it was time to expand again. My lack of desire to see people working for sixty cents an hour coupled with my strong desire to make money led me to the following experiment.

If I don't have to deal with finding, hiring, and then training individual workers, that means, well, not having to do anything I just mentioned. Perfect! So I asked my soon-to-be "manager" if he knew other "good people" at his former place of employment that might be interested in a job with us. He immediately said YES! I tasked him with finding two potential contractors, and told him to have them contact me. He did exactly that, a man and woman. After a short messaging session on Skype, I liked both. Before offering them a job, I talked to the soon-to-be manager about the hiring process, meaning the customs or other stuff involved. His response was mildly unsettling. He told me, with no hesitation, that we should offer the woman half of what we offered the man, and that was just how it worked there. That was my first real wakeup call to the cultural differences. Needless to say, I didn't do that. I gave both the same offer I gave to my now-manager, and gave him a 33 percent raise, while also educating him on why sexism wasn't going to exist within the confines of our company.

DECISION TIME—ALL YOU CAN DO IS ALL YOU CAN DO

Before we get back to conquering the Internet, I need to once again bring up the fact that I remained a student.

With all of this exciting, yet distracting business stuff going on, I unsurprisingly had a really poor semester. In fact, I had to withdraw from several courses after falling too far behind. Feeling disappointed, embarrassed, and wasteful for enrolling in and paying for courses that I wasn't passing (and was even quitting) weighed upon me. After all, I was fairly close to finishing. However, the required courses ahead had a reputation of being brutal.

What to do?

So I went back to the Pros and Cons exercise and came to the conclusion that I could always re-enroll in school. I also realized I might be onto something really profitable. What I knew without a doubt was that I wasn't likely to succeed at both. So I quit school. It was a really tough decision, but I justified that I only went back to school to learn exactly what I was doing. And that is how I dropped out of the fifth college I attended. No regrets.

What happened next solidified that decision as the correct one.

PAUL, ANGELA, AND JUSTIN BIEBER, TOO!

What we were doing in Cebu City with our blogging allowed us to publish what I will just define as an "insane" number of blog articles. These, coupled with our ticket buying and reselling, were producing significant revenue and profits. At this point, the Million Dollar Bedroom had been born. We were definitely producing well over a million dollars in revenue annually.

Was this enough for me? Of course not. There was one thing truly lacking. Previously, I explained the "Long Tail." Well, we were without a doubt absolutely dominating that. When I would introduce myself on the phone to other ticket resellers, they immediately knew who we were. Most had either had a sale directed to them from our site (TicketNetwork Partner Program) or saw us all over their last Google search. So why was I feeling incomplete?

I wanted to escape the long tail. I wanted it all. I wanted to be at the top for any and all searches. (Insert the sound of a diabolical laugh here.) So I went back into mad scientist, *Castaway* mode. It took me about a month, but I figured it out.

Earlier, I gave you a brief explanation of the way search engines worked at the time—how links that pointed to your website (coupled with what those links said) had a big impact on your site's search engine ranking. Basically, I needed more links to my site with very specific text on those links. But even back then, this wasn't super easy, as credible and authoritative sites don't just let you create links to your site saying whatever you want. So I continued my search.

What I am about to share I am not particularly proud of, nor am I suggesting you do it. I came across a method of link creation that more or less let you do whatever you wanted. Finding a site with some authority that allowed you to create an outbound link was not only time consuming, it was also sometimes really hard to do at all. This is when I found what was referred to as "Paul and Angela" links. These links, named after the original publisher of lists of them, were placed in the "Bio" section of popular websites that let you create a profile. So you might join the fan club of a popular musician and then be able to have a profile page on the site. In the "About Me" or "Bio" section, all you had to do was add the HTML for 2–3 links that might say "Justin Bieber tickets" or "concert tickets" or whatever. At the time, these links not only counted, but also were really powerful. Why? Well, most of these sites were pretty reputable. How could you find out which sites allow this? Good ol' Paul and Angela published a new list for you each month. As long as you paid your monthly subscription, you would get your list. That being said, the unknowing websites that were about to be overwhelmed with these very much unwanted new users often quickly caught on and either deleted the profiles or closed the ability to add them.

My new army of online workers was now not only able to publish blogs, but they could also produce a whole lot of these links. It worked. I mean *really* worked. Over the next couple of months, we saw our search engine rankings SKYROCKET. I will give one example. I mentioned the term "Justin Bieber tickets." If you don't already know, good old JB is a popular dude. As a result of what we had done, we had risen to number one for the search term "Justin Bieber tickets." Do you know how hard this is? Now imagine the potential value. At the time that we occupied this space, he never announced a tour; however, we still averaged anywhere from 500–1000 visits *a day* to that page. I remember having legitimate concern about what would or could happen if he announced a tour. I thought it would probably crash the server, which would mean we couldn't collect the Justin Bieber sales, and we would also miss out on all of our normal daily sales coming in, too.

We rode this gravy train of search engine glory through the end of 2010 and into 2011. I'm not going to tell you what this was worth, but I will tell you that it was a lot. I knew that I had crossed a line. By that, I mean that I wasn't really operating ethically. I also knew that it probably wasn't likely to last. And I was, in fact, about to learn my lesson.

Killed by a Panda

Here we are in early 2011. Having not taken a vacation for quite some time, I bought Jill and myself a trip to St. Thomas in the US Virgin Islands. I sat on a beach watching the website sales roll in. One distinct memory was that the *daily* income related to these sales was enough to cover the entire cost of the trip. After basking in the sun and my feeling of genius for being able to make money on vacation, something odd happened on the last day. Our sales were down—in fact, so far down that we were barely making any. Since our time in St. Thomas was up, we headed back to Indianapolis.

Upon arriving home, I realized that I had been killed by a Panda. So how am I writing this book? Well, it wasn't a real panda. It was an update to Google's search algorithm called "Panda," which seemed to punish sites with weak content.

How did I even know? It was pretty easy to figure out once several days of poor sales started lining up. So I looked at our search traffic. What was going on? Did we really just lose 90 percent of our traffic? I started researching online and found lots of people complaining about the same thing. Maybe it was a mistake. The next day came and I'd lost 95 percent of my traffic. This wasn't good. How could this be happening?! So more looking online and now people are starting to figure it out. Google caught on. The jig was up. It was likely they were penalizing sites, most of which seemed to be loaded with content that was either duplicate or repetitive.

I felt sick to my stomach. No joke there, I remember feeling like I could puke everywhere. What had I done? Surely this could be fixed, right? Another few days passed. Now I'm down to less than one percent of the traffic I had a week prior. The graph displaying my web traffic looked like the price of Enron stock during that fiasco.

As the traffic slowed, so did the income. That is the way of the world. Over the coming months, I tried everything—including deleting the excessive number of pages we had created through our blogging activities. That didn't help. The penalty was so severe that it killed the ranking of the other pages we had driven to the top of search, despite the fact that it was only designed to detect duplicate content. If your site caught this penalty, the reality was it affected everything.

At the time, I had no backup. This was my only ticket site. My traffic and revenue were now pitiful. All of the work we had done up to this point was gone. Nothing I did brought the site back to life. It appeared that anyone, meaning any website assessed with this penalty, wasn't able to recover. It seemed to be a true kiss of death.

This left me in a bit of a pickle. I had hired all of these workers and programmers, and then my revenue around it disappeared. I needed to figure something out fast.

So with a major source of my revenue having dried up, but my expenses staying constant, it became apparent that I was going to need to make some changes. I was now questioning my decision to buy out my partner as well. While buying and selling tickets was still working out, some of the deals I made with sports teams and venues along the way required all of the cash we had on hand. My cash flow was really becoming problematic. It wasn't that we didn't have any money; it just wasn't in the places we needed it to be. See, if you buy a bunch of season tickets from a venue or a sports team, you have to pay them up front. This is usually far in advance. It meant I had to wait to receive the tickets in order to deliver them, which meant that I also needed to wait to get paid. All problematic.

MILLION DOLLAR LESSON: Learn to be aware of the life cycle of your cash. If it takes a long time to sell something that you paid for in advance, then that is a slow life cycle. You can also use "Turn Ratio" to be more scientific about it.

In order to cut my expenses, I let the intern go. Yes, I know earlier I told you that he ended up working with us for years. Still true—you will hear more about that later. But at that time, I was questioning sustainability and he was graduating from a top school that same year. I figured he was probably going to end up with a better job somewhere else soon anyway.

In addition, my original office manager sensed instability and moved on to work at the Hilton. I didn't try to talk her out of it. Then it was just Jill and me in the original Million Dollar Bedroom. It's really interesting how quickly your dynamic can change. Not long before, it seemed like I was going to need to use some of the money we had made to build another bedroom on the house just to have a place to put another desk. Now Jill was the office manager and I still had a whole lot of contractors in the Philippines.

MILLION DOLLAR LESSON: Sometimes you learn more from your mistakes than your successes. If you haven't made many yet, you will. Meaning, don't become overly confident. It's dangerous.

Learning to Adapt

I had done well, at least on paper. I felt like I was temporarily stuck waiting to get my cash back out of some of the contracts I had made with teams and venues. I did have a much lighter expense structure, but I also had a lot less help. I feared I was going to have to drop even more weight from my payroll. By that, I mean either Jill (local) or my contractors in the Philippines (overseas). I really didn't want to do that. With our overseas office, I had learned how remarkably helpful it could be to have that kind of workforce available. In fact, I had a huge advantage if I could just figure something out.

So back into mad scientist mode. I dug deep. We didn't just have to sell tickets, right? So I kept looking and looking and looking. We tried a few things, all unsuccessfully. Then I noticed something. I felt kind of dumb for not thinking of it sooner. Remember how we created our first online sale through posting ads on Craigslist? Well, that isn't what we went back to, largely because Craigslist will just kill your ads if you post too many. Yes, I know this because we did try that first. But what we found in its place was even better.

We know the three magic words in marketing are test, test, and test. So that is exactly what I did. Using the exact same templates from our blog, we started posting online classified ads on just about any classified site we could find. Why not? I did have a whole lot of people sitting in Cebu waiting for something to do.

95

Now I'd like to tell you what I discovered was intentional, but it wasn't. But it was impressive. In the process of testing a zillion different classified ad sites, I almost immediately noticed something. There was one site where, when we placed our ads, those ads then showed up in Google search. But whatever worked was fine with me. So let's see what happens when we try and step this up a notch.

MILLION DOLLAR LESSON: In business, you will be forced to adapt at some point. This is often what determines if you stay in business long term. Don't fight it, embrace it. Not doing so will result in your inability to stay open.

Scaling Back Up with Repurposed Technology

In the process of creating way too many blogs, we had created a whole lot of templates. Using these same templates, and the same people who had been publishing blogs, we started working on posting more online ads. I had to roll up my sleeves and really get into trying to figure out a new process for doing this. The ad site didn't seem to care about the volume of ads, meaning they weren't removing them if we posted a lot. Okay, that makes things easier. However, with multiple people posting the ads, there were some issues with overlap. Our communication was poor. So I had our programmer build us a simple online calendar that allowed me to put what events, tours, teams, or venues the workers should post ads for. We saw immediate improvement.

MILLION DOLLAR LESSON: If a team can't communicate, then they can't be efficient.

Over the next couple of months, I saw our sales slowly return. It wasn't anywhere near what it was before, but we quickly became profitable on that side of the business again. I felt a lot better. However, I noticed something. Each worker could only post about 10–11 ads per hour. That was about the same speed at which we could publish blog articles, but since these classified ads weren't as effective, it wasn't the same return on effort. If I could only figure out a way to speed that up.

I GOT IT! We could use the same process that we used to create web pages to make the templates! Back to mad scientist mode. This one started slowly, but after a few weeks I had it.

I just mentioned that a worker could post 10–11 ads per hour. This was largely due to the time it took to insert all of the variables into the different places within the template. Now that we could make these templates without needing to manually change all of the variables, it should be remarkably faster to put these ads out there. So we started doing some tests. The results were shocking. In the testing process, our output went up four times. Then after a week, once everyone really got it, it went up to five times the original output—meaning we could place about 50–55 ads per hour. We're back!

Better, faster, cheaper, right? I had all three. Now off to the races and making sales again. But first I had to deal with another issue. The slow cash flow and waiting for some of my ticket deals to mature had taken its toll on my ticket resale business. In fact, it was crap. I had spent so much time and energy focusing on fixing my website sales that I had basically ignored the thing that got me started in the business in the first place—buying and selling tickets.

Coin Toss Moment

Every business has a point when they face a big turning point. Essentially, it's when they decide how much longer, if at all, they can continue doing what they do. My business at the time was like a seesaw. One side went up, the other went down. I had done well so far. I was in a position where I could walk away with a decent chunk of change. I could let the workers in Cebu continue what they were doing and *still* be making good money. However, I needed to make a decision about the ticket resale thing. It was really cash intensive. By that, I mean it seemed like it was really going to take a lot of it to make it work on anything other than a scale that would provide a good but not remarkable living.

Now I'm going to sound like a jerk to some of you when I say this: I didn't start my own business to make the same low-six-figure income I had made before I went back to school. I started my own business because I wanted to get rich. Sorry, it's the truth. So while I was doing well enough to justify continuing, at the same time, the stress was definitely a factor. So was the potential risk of owning the company. Getting off to such a hot start made me feel somewhat bulletproof. As it turns out, I wasn't.

One morning I discussed it all with Jill. I think I knew that I was going to continue with the business, but I really did say, "How about we flip a coin? Heads we keep doing this, tails we don't and I go get a job."

She looked at me like I was nuts. "Isn't owning businesses what you always wanted to do?"

Needless to say, the coin never left my pocket.

All in all, my point is pretty simple. Make sure that you consider what you have on the line. Don't assume that every day will be sunny. And also be realistic about what you are going to undertake. Failure is part of the game. As long as you learn from it, you can become even better at what you do. Just understand that, on some level, at some time, you *will* experience it.

Small Business Funding

Having decided to continue what we were doing, there was still an issue to be addressed. Funding! I feel like I should quickly address something. Banks don't give loans to brand new businesses or ones that haven't been operating long. I think this is a common misperception. In fact, your bank is likely to want you to have anywhere from five to ten times in assets for every dollar they possibly loan you. Meaning, you might need $100,000 in assets just to get a $10,000–20,000-dollar credit line.

Why are these lending standards so fierce? The answer is simple: Because most new businesses fail. In fact, overwhelmingly. Roughly 80 percent of non-franchise new businesses fail within two years. This is actually why franchise models are so popular. So, in the event that you thought your funding was coming this way, let me be clear! You aren't getting a loan from a bank to start your business unless you have a whole lot of assets. And if you already have deep pockets, then you probably don't need the loan.

LEVERAGE

What I am about to explain is risky. In no way am I recommending that you do this. Why? Because if done improperly, or if things don't go your way, you might end up paying for it for a remarkably long time. This practice is known as "leveraging." It's actually a pretty common practice, but that doesn't mean it's not risky.

To leverage things in the business world means that you are using one thing to prop up or push forward another—usually when it comes to finances or funding. If done properly, it's powerful. If done incorrectly, it can be an absolute disaster. Extreme examples of failed leveraging include parts of the "Housing Bubble" from 2008 and on. When buyers took loans to purchase rental homes, they were using leverage. Essentially, homebuyers were using (or leveraging) the banks' money to finance loans on homes they only intended to rent out. Later, when the prices began to fall, many were stuck behind these loans, unable to pay them off, as the assets were now worth far less than what they owed (the liability associated with the loan).

For a much more reasonable, and possibly understandable explanation, I'll explain my situation. At the start of the company, I got others involved in my business by using their credit cards to purchase tickets that I later resold. This is an example of leveraging on a small scale. I used "OPM" or "Other People's Money" to purchase or fund something that I felt I would be able to turn for a profit. In some cases, like the one with my business partner, they actually owned part of my business. In other cases, I negotiated a small kicker or incentive for the use of their money, like giving them a payment of 1 percent of whatever I spent. This, plus the "points" or rewards that these cards often give, made the risk worth it for them. Had things gone poorly, my friends might have ended up being on the hook for whatever outstanding charges I was unable to pay. Same thing for myself in regards to my own credit lines.

Having found success with what I had already done, I felt confident enough to seek new forms of leverage when it came to my business.

The American Express Gold Card

If you already own a business, then you have most certainly received an offer from American Express. They really have a way of finding you when you register a new business entity. In doing so, they offer use of their Gold Card. This can either be the greatest thing ever or your kiss of death. Why? Well, this isn't a standard credit card where you'll accrue interest charges if you have a balance remaining after your grace period to repay. A *charge card*—like AmEx's Gold Card—requires the user to repay the *full outstanding balance* within thirty days of the statement being issued. Not doing so results in some steep fees. Since terms often change and they have different programs, you will need to check with them for details. That being said, if you get offered one of these cards, then decide to go forward using it, make sure that you understand what it is, and more importantly, know that you will have the ability to repay it that fast.

Having recently received these offers, I went ahead and applied and was approved. They used the term "No Preset Spending Limit." Seriously? I have an unlimited amount of credit? I found that to be interesting, and then began using it efficiently.

Utilizing this card, I was now able to deal with most of my short-term cash flow issues. I also found myself able to pump a lot more inventory into my business. Yes, I had to do so responsibly, however the impact was immediate. As I continued using my account, I pushed more and more purchases through the card. With the new spending power, I was able to negotiate some bulk deals with teams and venues. Since these events were often occurring quickly, I knew that I would have the ability to collect the money fast enough to pay American

Express back. But not all of the deals and purchases went well. In fact, I had a few that more or less blew up in my face. That is why this approach can be *really risky*. If you make bad purchases and end up selling at a loss, you will have to find the money for your AmEx payments elsewhere. In some cases, you might have slow-moving inventory, which can in some instances be worse than selling at a loss. Fortunately, we had enough good ones to overcome the bad.

All in all, things really turned the corner thanks to this new form of financing. The websites were profitable again, I was able to fund our short-term purchases without too much stress, and everything seemed great! I even called our former intern and begged him to come back full time, which he did. Life was grand once again…until one day in the spring of 2012.

I can't recall the exact day, or even month. I just know it was in early 2012. The phone rang and it was someone in the risk mitigation department at AmEx. Due to the high volume of my purchases, and sometimes outstanding balance, they wanted to do some auditing. I immediately knew this was going to be problematic, and I asked them, "Why bother me?" After all, I had never been late on a payment, or even close. I actually felt like I was a model client. The guy on the phone explained that since my outstanding balances sometimes went as high as $100,000, I had triggered the need for an audit. Again, I asked, "Was this truly necessary?" I mean, wasn't this a card with no preset spending limit? Apparently not.

The reason this was going to be a problem was that they requested our last three years of tax returns, balance sheets, profit and loss reports, and a strand of my DNA (I'm kidding about that last part). I knew I was in trouble, as I didn't readily have all of that available. And more importantly, having been in business for such a short period of time, I figured that they would average the three years to make a decision regarding the usage of the card. And I had roughly two weeks to return the information.

I called my accountant in a mild panic. We had just spent a whole lot of time getting the books straight. I'll get to that soon. The previous year had easily been our best, however it was still early in the year. We hadn't even prepared to file our tax return yet. If I returned just the previous two years to American Express, I would be giving them information most likely used to make a decision that wasn't to my advantage (since it would be based on only the first two years of business, which weren't as impressive). Let me put it this way, no business in their first two years has books that they would like to be judged on. Regardless, the clock was ticking and I was seriously leveraged in regards to this account.

What if they placed a limit on it, or shut it off altogether?

A Ball of Rubber Bands

Let's jump back in the timeline just a bit in order to get back to the American Express situation. In the spring of 2011, I had to request an extension when it came to filing my taxes. Why? Because my books were a disaster. Not in regards to the profits, but due to something I had done early in the life of the business. At the time, I was then putting in any kind of money I had available in order to get things going, or keep them going. These funds often came from my own "personal" money. Meaning, I would sometimes give myself a paycheck, then turn around and put it back into the business. Also, since the business was in my home, I sometimes paid my bills with company funds, sometimes not. This is referred to as "comingling." Is it a problem? If you are a sole proprietor, it isn't a huge problem because you and your business aren't separate entities. However, if you formed some kind of business entity, it is in fact an issue.

I knew along the way that I was comingling my funds. And I knew I shouldn't do it, but I continued anyway. My thought process was that I would figure it out later.

MILLION DOLLAR LESSON: If you say that you will "figure it out later," know that you will in fact have to do this. Doing things the way they SHOULD be done is the easier approach, both for now *and* later.

Well, if I had to "figure it out later," then later had certainly arrived. By the way, if you're ever around my accountant, avoid mentioning this subject. Doing so will likely result in feeling like your life is in danger. But getting back to the AmEx audit, our poor early accounting standards coupled with my comingling had created what seemed like a ball of rubber bands now in need of untangling. The process took six weeks.

A Smashed Phone, Some Cursing, and the Feeling of "Oh Sh*t!"

Having just gone through accounting hell, I now found myself dialing my accountant again to unleash an urgent surprise. After I explained what American Express had called about, and what they wanted, we then spent a few minutes doing some mild cursing. After what sounded like old sailors that just left port, we decided that we would need to get to work the next day.

Much to our surprise, we made significant progress on bringing our books up to speed for the prior year. The following day we finished it. We were now able to file a tax return and provide American Express with the complete documents they wanted. Nonetheless, I knew I still had a problem. In the first year of the business, we didn't have a lot of revenue. We had more in the second year; however, when we switched over to the affiliate-based system with TicketNetwork, we no longer had the same revenue structure. We were now only collecting the fees associated with the orders, not the entire sale. While that benefitted the business as a whole, it didn't benefit the revenue we were able to represent. So, while our profitability was still there overall, our revenue wasn't as high as I felt American Express would like it to be. It is what it is, I thought, so I went ahead and uploaded the files they had requested.

A few days later I received a phone call. The guy on the line informed me that they were putting a $60,000 limit on the card. Despite having always paid them on time, they were going to cap me. My earlier assumption was, in fact, correct; the past history of the business and everything they looked at was averaged over a three-year period. Those early years were haunting the average. In addition, I was leveraging the card pretty hard. I had about $80,000 outstanding at the time of the call. So wait? *I need to give them $20,000 right now just to only then still be maxed?* I tried to persuade the guy to reach another decision. He didn't care one bit and the call ended.

As I hung up, I was so insanely upset that I immediately spiked the phone onto my hardwood floor as if I had just scored a touchdown. Let's put it this way. We were finding tiny pieces of that phone over the next year. I'm embarrassed for scaring the crap out of everyone at the office and for acting like a child.

The result of American Express's decision was an immediate problem. I knew that I could come back from it; however, until we collected some money, it was going to really slow us down. To this day, on some level, I'm still upset about it. In fact, after paying that card back, I refused to even use it for quite some time. At the end of that same year, and after filing my taxes, I requested that the same department review my numbers. They doubled my limit.

MILLION DOLLAR LESSON: Don't run things too tight. It's easy to want to put your cash back into new purchases and avenues to make money; however, it is really important to keep cash on hand too, just in case you need it.

Amidst all of the fervor and drama that American Express had caused, something really great occurred. I made my last payment to my former partner. It really was an amazing feeling. It was also an incredible feeling to no longer have to send monthly checks. I felt as if I had just received a sizable raise! Probably because I had.

Soapy Bubbles

After sending the last payment to my partner, things really took off. As much as I'd like to detail that, overall it's somewhat boring. I mean outside of the fact that we made a bunch of money, paid a bunch of taxes, and then decided to make some really big changes. In May of 2013, Jill and I got married. Just before the wedding, Jill gave me the task of dropping off our two dogs at the groomer/doggie hotel. We were getting married in St. Thomas in a few days, and these hounds needed to be in a good place before we left the next morning.

The dog groomer was located about twenty minutes from where we lived. The business was owned by a lady I had known for a while, and I had remained a loyal customer despite this distance. Since I was pretty much busy all day and night, I tried calling before I left. No answer. I waited about ten minutes and called again. Still no answer. Did I miss them? So I went to the website, which was not much help except that the hours of operation indicated that they were supposedly open. It sure didn't seem like it.

At this point, I was admittedly annoyed—mostly with myself for waiting until the very last minute, then embarking on a twenty-minute one-way drive to see if the place was even open. If they weren't, I was in a different kind of trouble, as our flight left really early. I truly didn't want to have to tell Jill that I dropped the ball on the only task I was given to prepare for our trip. Yeah, I know.

About two minutes into the drive, my mind started racing. I thought, *Why wasn't I able to finalize this reservation online?* Then I continued on my mental rant. *Our developers could probably build something that would allow that.* Halfway there and still concerned that I really messed up, I moved on from the mental rant straight into talking to myself. If it helps your overall picture of me, then maybe I was talking to the dogs. However, they probably didn't hear much given the fact that their heads were hanging out the window.

I'm almost to the groomer now. Time for the big reveal. I pulled up…and they're there. Thank god this was going to end well.

So into the groomer/dog hotel I went. When I got inside, there wasn't anyone upfront. Who cares—at least they're open! I'm off the hook on that at least. After about a minute of waiting, I heard a voice from the back of the building yell "I'm back here!" So I headed toward the back room. Passing through the doorway, I had all of my answers. In front of me was a lady with a giant, wet dog—both somewhat covered in bubbles. I chuckled because it was kind of funny, then I told her how happy I was that she was in fact there. She apologized and told me that it was impossible to answer the phone due to bubble overload and her helper wasn't there. I then gave her a couple more dogs to deal with and went on my way.

Most people having just avoided a situation where they didn't have to tell their soon-to-be wife that they had failed at the only task given to them before leaving on a momentous trip would have been happy with that and moved on. Not me. In fact, I got right back into talking to myself as I just admitted that I sometimes do. I thought about how much business that place probably misses out on from not answering the phone. Why couldn't it all be done online? There has to be someone that does this, right? I couldn't get the image of the soapy, bubble-covered dog and groomer out of my head.

As I continued my drive, the conversation with myself picked up. "We have built calendars. We have built reminders!" I said this as if I were speaking to a room full of my peers. "Can it really be that hard to take a booking online?"

I finally arrived home and immediately told Jill that I had a brilliant idea! I will omit her response a few days before our wedding, but I'll allude to the fact that she was excited at the prospect of hearing about it for the next week. Okay, it didn't play out like that, but I really want you to like Jill! So after listening to me go on and on for quite a while, I finally calmed down and went to bed ready to go to a tropical island and marry my dream girl.

A few days later, I got married on a beach with a small handful of friends, family, and co-workers present. However, I couldn't get the online appointment stuff out of my head. Since Jill had in fact already said "I Do," I felt as if it was okay to really chatter on and on about it. The more I thought about it, the more I realized that anyone not using appointment-booking technology was certainly going to soon anyway.

On the plane ride back to Indianapolis, I filled up four cocktail napkins with possible domain names. It was becoming pretty clear to me that this idea wasn't going away any time soon.

Upon returning to Indianapolis, I went to pick up my dogs. While there, I asked the business owner if she had ever considered an online reservation system. She said she had, but quickly dismissed it because of the cost. So I put the dogs in the car, drove home, and got back to work with my normal activities. But every moment I had free, I kept looking into the online booking industry. There were definitely players in the market. Most of them had a fairly high price too. Then I saw the signal flare.

In the spring of 2012, Intuit, best known for accounting software, had purchased DemandForce for

$423,000,000. Wait, *what?* Yes, 423 *million* dollars. That was about all I needed to dive in headfirst. I figured that if a company like Intuit was putting that kind of money into something, then they clearly saw the future for that industry.

The following month, Jill and I picked up our entire company and moved it to Kansas City, which is my hometown. That doesn't have much to do with my newfound obsession with online appointment booking, but I do really need to mention it because…

We were finally leaving the Million Dollar Bedroom!

At this point, this was very much a welcome thing. It had become pretty tight in there. So we packed up the truck and headed west. Our longtime intern, then full-time employee, elected to stay in Indianapolis. We didn't fully realize what a big loss that was until later, but we will get into that shortly.

Overall, things were strong for the two years up to that point. That being said, all good things do come to an end. By that, I mean our online marketing efforts finally died down. Of course, they did so right around the time we moved, as if we didn't have enough on our plates. Certain changes to the way Google viewed the ads we placed reduced their relevance and therefore reduced the associated traffic. The sales went shortly thereafter. Not long after that, I had to let go of several of the people that had been posting those ads for us. I felt terrible. I had really come to know most of these folks, and had played a big role in helping them provide a better life for themselves. And in turn they really did the same for us.

While we had just made some pretty serious changes to our personnel overseas, we did keep four people in the office there: two programmers and two general online helpers. These were the very first people who would work on what would later become the biggest project I have ever participated in.

PLANNING? WHAT'S THAT?

At this point in my life, I hadn't really learned to appreciate the value of a thorough plan. I used to just jump and then build wings. It's not the correct way to do things, but it is the way I often times approached things. Can't do much about that now.

So off we went, ready to try and build the basics of an online appointment-booking site that still didn't have a name or a domain. I started by reviewing all of the things that we had built along the way. Some of the proprietary things included an online calendar that allowed for data entry. We used this to enter names of artists or events for which we wanted to post ads. Also within the tools that we had created was a notification system to make it easier when it came to alerting our customers that their tickets were about to ship. Beyond that we didn't really have a whole lot else.

Now I know I told you that at the time I wasn't a big planner. I did, however, sit down and write out the basic functions that I felt this new concept needed to perform. I also found the competition at the time and got into their systems in order to get a better idea of what existed in the marketplace. I then sent all of these requirements to our head programmer in Cebu City and asked how long he thought it would take to build all of this. He told me six months. Sounds great, I thought, let's get started!

A Conservation with
General Homes Founder and CEO
Jim Olafson

I've had the pleasure of knowing Jim Olafson for my entire life. How? He's my uncle. Married to my mother's sister, Uncle Jim as I know him has a remarkable history as a businessperson and, on top of that, is a heck of a role model for anyone who appreciates work ethic, integrity, and modesty. Over the years, he's provided keen insight that I've used to help find my own success in owning and operating businesses.

In 1973, Jim Olafson founded General Homes, a Texas-based housing company. After working in the construction industry for years, he decided the time was right to start doing it for himself. The events that followed were remarkable, turbulent, and filled with a lot of great learning opportunities—which Jim has graciously shared during our conversation. But first, let me create a basic timeline for you.

1973—General Homes is founded.
1978—General Homes is sold for $24 million.
1981—Jim Olafson retires from company but stays on board of directors.

1983—Company is purchased back from buyer for $32 million.

1983—General Homes goes public with shares starting at nineteen dollars. $60 million in stock is sold during its initial public offering.

1988—Company encounters financial difficulty and declares bankruptcy.

1988—At the request of creditors, Jim Olafson returns to "fix" the company.

1998—Company is sold to Kaufman and Broad.

MATT: Your company grew pretty fast. Did you take any particular approach?

JIM: Well, first I sat down and wrote a five-year game plan of where I wanted to be. You need a road map to follow. It's much easier if you set some goals. I said, "We're going to have this many subdivisions, this many people, and do this much volume." It's pretty simple when you've got to follow the dots.

What are some of the things you had to learn fast as you started the business?

I think the thing that overwhelmed me the most was the financial part because my background was in construction. Finance is something you either have to learn or hire someone who knows a hell of a lot about it.

What are the best or most useful things you could tell someone who is starting a business?

Hire good people. And have a lot of integrity. We wrote a personnel policy. People like to know where they stand in a company and if the company stands behind them. The integrity part is to say *here's what we're going to do* and then *do it.* If you tell them you're going to pay them, you pay them. You're going to give them however many vacations days, insurance, etc. But you expect something in return. It's a two-way street. They give us a certain amount of work, loyalty, and expertise, and we give them a certain amount of benefits, money, and so forth. That's part of the game and you have to honor it.

The other part of integrity is if you're going to build a product, you have to service it. Houses are not going to be perfect. They're going to have problems and you have to take care of those problems. Some builders have bad reputations of never servicing, never fixing…but they don't stay in business very long.

In regards to hiring good people, you said, "I always hired people who are smarter than me."

We tested everybody that I hired. That's *everyone* in the company—from a janitor to a president. They had to pass an IQ test. And we didn't hire anybody unless they were in the 95th percentile in intelligence. And then we tested them psychologically. We had three hundred questions and answers. There was a certain psychological profile that seemed to fit best in our environment. And by testing, that's the type of people we tried to hire. Also, smart people.

I once thought there were only two reasons why people don't do what you want them to do: 1) they don't know how or 2) they don't care. Years later, I realized there was a third: they just *can't*. When you hire smart people, you know they aren't dumb. You know they can figure it out. Now if they don't care, there's nothing you can do but get rid of them.

One thing I always say to business owners is there's a moment when you realize your employees will never care as much as you do. Do you have any thoughts on that?

The definition of management is getting people to do what you want them to do. It's a part of the equation. If you can get them to see it as in their own best interest, then you have a leg up on this thing. The people we hired were always on a career path. They wanted to accomplish and to be successful. If you can get *those* people, you don't have to kick them in the butt or stick them with a cattle prod. You'd like to have to rein them in, not spur 'em on.

Was there anything you did or learned that helped facilitate that?

I think it's just by trial and error. Everybody is different. You learn with each individual you manage what is the best method. And if you want somebody to change, *you* have to change. That's true in managing kids or people or anything. You can't just treat everyone the same. You have to focus on what makes *them* motivated. That's the game and what's interesting about it.

When you said you were looking for a certain profile of people, I understand the intelligence part, but once you get past that, you can be intelligent but not be driven. Or you can be unintelligent but have a hell of a lot of drive. Was there a specific personality trait past intelligence that you guys sought?

Getting the intelligence is simple. It's just numbers. That's a brain thing. The next thing is their personality— it's what gives them drive. Did they have a paper route when they were a kid? Or did they join the Boy Scouts? Do they like to lead or to follow? These are the kinds of things you look for when you do the personality tests. Are they impetuous? Or are they hostile? And there's a range to consider. If you're too impetuous, that's not good. But if you're not impetuous at all, that's not good either, as you'll never be able to make a decision. And you have to have some hostility because you must be able to fire people or tell someone no. But you can't have so much hostility that you're abrasive, as that will kill any initiative. So there's a balance in all these things. And over the years we figured out—as best as one can— what type of personality fit our type of operation.

When you realized you held stock worth millions at one point, and then later it's worth nothing due to whatever reasons, what goes through your head? Was there regret?

Oh sure. Anytime anything unfavorable happens you wish you'd done something different. I mean, if you're driving a nail and you hit your thumb, you'll wish you hadn't done that because it hurts. There are a lot of things I'd have done differently, but that's the past. The future is you have to get on your horse and go get it back.

One of the things I've always admired is your work ethic. Can you share a few things about your approach?

I think that's just the way you're born. If you don't have integrity and character by the time you're six, seven, or eight years old, you're not going to get it when you're twenty-five. If you don't have it at that early age, sorry.

Was that something that was taught to you? Was your dad like that?

Yeah, my dad had a strong work ethic. He went to work even when he could barely walk due to a bad back. He believed he *had* to go to work. He worked since he was a kid. But I worked since I was a kid, too. I sold mistletoe when I was six years old. Maybe the way you're raised has some part of it. I don't know what percent—10, 20,

30? The rest I think you're simply born with…just like blue eyes or brown hair.

Is there anything else that you'd like to add for people wanting to improve or start up a business?

The biggest thing they should do is research. And I don't care what business it is—you've got to research the market. The whole thing. The more research they do, the more successful they'll be.

SECTION THREE:

LESSONS TO LEARN BEFORE STARTING THE NEXT BIG THING

HAVING SECURED some financial success, Jill and I purchased a much larger home in Kansas City. You might think we would go ahead and relocate the business to an office. Nope, we basically moved it into the Million Dollar Basement. We specifically found a home that had a basement with a full walk-out and ten-foot ceiling. The only problem—we didn't have any employees who lived in the same city as us. Mentioning this to Jill, she wisely replied, "How long do you think that is going to last?" We both knew that it wouldn't be long.

Are There *Any* .coms Left?

As we moved forward in our attempt to create an MVP (minimally viable product) for our new booking platform, there remained an issue. We still didn't have a name or a domain to go with it. If you've never looked for domain names and you feel like you need some cheap entertainment, do the following. Visit GoDaddy.com or any online registrar where you can register a domain name, then create a fictional company in your head. Now see how many tries it takes you to find a suitable (and available) dot com to go with it. Come back when you're done.

One hour later...

Pretty crazy, right? How can that be? Are so many web domains really already registered? YES, THEY ARE!

Mark Twain famously said, "Buy land, they're not making it anymore." A similar quote is often contributed to Will Rogers. Since I really don't know who that is, let's stick with Mark Twain. This adage was true for a really long time until one thing happened—THE INTERNET.

The growing presence of the Internet, and then the shift to online commerce, created a whole new form of "real estate." You might think virtual real estate is not the same, but let me ask, would you rather own the domain name "cars.com" or the quarter acre of dirt that your house sits on? Unless you live in a prime spot in Manhattan or downtown San Francisco, you should probably go with the domain name. In fact, I'd wager you should go with it in every instance.

Once entire businesses, stores, and communities formed online, the virtual places in which this commerce occurred became a valuable form of real estate. Much like acquiring or trading land, speculators, brokers, and investors came along. And *that* is the reason you can't usually find the domain name you want available. Someone else beat you to it. They are either holding it for whatever reason OR they have it up for sale in a number of places, waiting for someone like you to decide it's worth paying a premium to claim.

So what are some of the things to look for when buying a domain name? Well, in some cases, this is also going to be your company name, so there's that. Another thing to strongly consider is the length. Shorter is better. Thisisthelongestdomainnamepossible.com is not a good choice. The general rule I prefer to use is if it's too many characters before the .com to be a twitter handle, then it's too long.

Here are some other useful rules and guidelines I personally consider:

Try to stick with .com suffixes. Most people expect it and thus will be their default when trying to recall your domain name.

Avoid hyphens, numbers, and phonetic or clever spelling. Otherwise, you will figure out quickly that you have to clearly define this to EVERYONE.

Example: "What's your website again?"

"Yoga4u.com. That's Yoga, the number four, the letter U dot com."

See what I mean? It's annoying for all parties (and undoubtedly will send some potential customers to "yogaforyou.com").

Consider how words look when you crunch them together. What impression do they make? I typically try to avoid domains that put the same letter together too many times in a row. And be sure you don't accidentally spell weird, offensive, or embarrassing words.

Example: Comp**asswhole**salers.com

Another bit of advice is to visit your digital "neighbors." This means visiting the domains that might come up if—or inevitably *when*—someone either types in the wrong URL or something close but still not yours. The most notable example I can think of here is Dick's Sporting Goods. If you have ever decided to visit their site, you may have made the same mistake I once did and entered "dicks.com." If so, you may have noticed those men on the screen weren't playing basketball. Dick's Sporting Goods has since acquired that domain name; however, I imagine it wasn't cheap.

The final advice I have for you in regards to domain selection is to try and find a domain that has already been online for a while. It's a good idea if done properly for one reason. Search engine algorithms discount brand new domains. They do so in order to avoid those that will come along and use Black Hat SEO techniques to quickly pump up a domain, make some money from the great search positioning, only to then catch a penalty from the search engine, which results in them ditching the domain. So in order to avoid such practices, most popular search engines don't give you much "street cred" unless you have been on the street for a while.

And We Have a Winner

Realizing the importance of a domain name, my search went on for way too long. Then it finally fell in my lap. Sitting there one day looking through auction listings on GoDaddy I found GigaBook.com. PERFECT! The name was short, relevant, and modern. What was even better was that the asking price was only five hundred dollars. While that might seem like a lot to some of you, it's not. So I put in an offer and after a little back and forth I had myself a domain.

As quickly as we moved our rapidly evolving platform to this domain, I found an unanticipated issue. Despite the singular pronunciation of GigaBook, people really seemed to like calling it GigaBooks. How did I know this? Because two of the first five people I asked to visit the domain got it wrong and went to gigabooks.com! Then it got even more complicated. I realized that the phrase "GigaBook" had previously been used for a line of laptops! At this point, I felt pretty stupid. Did I not only just buy a domain that I don't own the plural for, but also bought one for a trademarked phrase?

After a call to my lawyer, who by the way charges $250 an hour, I felt better. He told me that since we were doing something completely different than the previous use of "GigaBook" that we should be fine. In addition, he pointed out that two terms as common as "giga" and "book" were not likely to draw a trademark. I specifically mentioned my lawyer's robust hourly rate because you can actually call a 1-900 number cheaper than $250 an hour. Yes, I'm going somewhere with this. The point that I am trying to make is that when you use professional services that are expensive, get to the point, and do it quickly. While I am normally cool with a little idle chitchat, when I call my lawyer that isn't ever the case.

Now feeling better that I wasn't about to build a company with the same name as a trademarked product, I still had the other issue of not owning GigaBooks.com. Using the "Who Is" registry, I figured out the owner of the domain and contacted them. After a little back and forth, I was able to purchase the domain for $1,500. Yep, *three times* what I paid for GigaBook.com. What I thought was a value ended up being fairly expensive. To this day, all GigaBooks.com does is forward to GigaBook.com. Let my loss be your gain when it comes to checking this stuff out ahead of time.

Before we move on, I do need to point out that I actually got fairly lucky when it came to the plural domain. Had I run into a situation where the domain owner was using it for something and didn't want to sell, that could have been bad. Another unwanted scenario would be if my project had significantly moved forward to the point of creating a noticeable or reputable product. If the owner of the similar domain recognized that, I could have been in a minor hostage situation. So the seller, knowing why and how badly I wanted this problem-causing domain, would be able to sharply increase its selling price.

How Tall Is the Ceiling in Here?

Sometimes, no matter how great you want to be at something, you will hit a ceiling. This is true mentally, physically, and in other ways too. I was about to learn a lot more about this roadblock.

As the winter months approached in 2013, so did a sticking point in our platform development. We had created a pretty terrible prototype. It was nothing I was willing to put my name on yet. And my current developers seemed maxed out. By this, I mean they reached a point of limitation when it came to what they could continue to build. Now don't get me wrong, my guys are good. However, this project seemed to be taking on a level of complexity that I hadn't expected.

At this point, we had created a basic calendar, the ability to input items on the calendar, and you could add clients and edit them. But the issue we had was that I wanted GigaBook users to be able to place something on their existing website that allowed their clients to schedule or request appointments on a real-time basis. Apparently, that was going to be A LOT harder than I anticipated. My team in Cebu had always figured things out—maybe not instantly, but as they would say, "We will find ways, Matt." This didn't appear to be the case here. I needed to figure something out or this project was about to get parked in Matt's Shipyard of Wrecked Projects. Which, by the way, isn't where you want to be docked.

Over the two years that followed, I learned a lot of lessons—many of which are based on expensive attempts to find the right people and processes needed to build and then maintain a successful company. While not all stories are the same, hopefully you can use mine to make yours even better.

The Startup Phenomenon

As the Internet grew, so did ambition. From the very beginning, people were making disgusting amounts of money. In fact, some were making money on business models that didn't even come close to panning out.

Since 2000, countless startups have received at least some amount of financing. Most failed. However, amongst all of that, you can still find a red-hot market filled with investment capital all looking for the same thing: a Home Run! This continues to be what drives investment into the next "big" thing.

So as we now get into the lessons that you need to learn on your way down the road, it will be up to you to decide how far you dare to travel. The road is filled with obstacles—so many that navigating through all of them is nearly impossible. I know, I'm starting to sound cynical. But I'm not; I'm just a realist. I actually wish I had been a lot more cynical about stuff along the way. I probably would have saved myself a lot of money. But we never really learn that a stove will burn us until we lay our hand on it at the wrong time.

Are you ready to begin creating *your* start-up destiny or Million Dollar Bedroom? Going forward, there are no more Million Dollar Lessons because everything to follow is a master class.

Is There Room in Here for All of Us?

It is estimated that there are currently more than one billion websites on the Internet as of early 2017. Not all of them are startup enterprises. Most aren't. However, with a number like that staring back at you, it's a good idea to first consider how much competition really exists out there. Not doing so is a one-way path to heartache.

So that all being said, the first thing you need to do is answer the following questions:

Who is my competition?

Who might become my competition?

Have I really searched high and low for potential competition?

Those sure do seem like really basic questions, right? Well they are. These are the very first building blocks when it comes to turning any business concept into something we can then start planning.

If you can't find any competition, then you need to ask yourself a couple more questions. It is important along the way that you answer questions like these with total honesty, not optimism.

If no one else is doing this, am I actually the first?

If no one else is doing this, is there actually a market?

The reason the answers to these questions are important is because you need to determine if what you are about to launch, build, or buy into does in fact have a market.

MARKET VIABILITY

To determine market viability means to establish what the real market for a product, service, or revenue-generating action is. Misjudging this is hugely problematic. Doing so is what leads to a warehouse filled with unsellable merchandise, countless hours of development into software products that no one wants, or possible products that are created blindly without a basic understanding of what competition they would be up against.

TARGET MARKET

The most basic element to first define is your general target market. This can be broad, such as "Web development companies," which will at least indicate an area of industry or consumer base that you want to target.

TARGET CUSTOMER

Next, you will need to be more specific by establishing a clearly defined customer. This must be far more specific than the target market answer. Identify examples of the kind of companies that you want to do business with. If you are planning on marketing something directly to consumers, who are they? Today's world of business is remarkably specific. In fact, it's so specific that you probably wonder how Facebook knows that you like a certain candy bar or product. Why should you care? Because it doesn't do much for you to spend time or money trying to sell stuff to those who aren't likely to buy it.

How Large Is the Potential Market for My Idea?

How many total consumers or businesses does your product have the potential to reach? This is a cornerstone of market viability. You don't necessarily have to reach the masses to be successful. Some even say, "There are riches in niches." However, if your product is very much a niche idea, then you need to be a lot more exact in your predictions. Smaller total market segments mean you have much less room for error, and you have less leeway when it comes to your reputation in that market. If you do manage to become the first in an industry, you can really do well.

So what is a decent or acceptable market size? The answer to that has huge variables based on what industry or consumer bases you intend to serve. When I started GigaBook, it was due to an amazingly large market segment that the platform could service. However, with that came more complexity. Rather than immediately being ready to go for a specific industry, we instead had to be highly customizable in order to appeal to such a large market segment. This meant more setup and customization was required. The result was some new users got overwhelmed, or gave up and never came back. So our strength and our weakness was the exact same thing.

What Benefits Does It Create for the User/Buyer?

Consumers don't buy features, they buy benefits. Benefits come in a number of different forms as listed below. It is important to really understand the benefits that your product or service will create for consumers or businesses. The fewer that exist, the harder it is to monetize. Ask yourself, are the benefits your product provides obvious? Meaning, will a consumer immediately know exactly what these are and how they'll benefit?

Here are some benefits that consumers look for when buying:

- Saves money
- Ease of use
- Creates efficiency
- Results in time savings
- Improves the status or image of the buyer
- Is perceived as a great overall value

If your idea doesn't provide any of the benefits I just listed, then it's likely that you are going to have a difficult time monetizing it. That doesn't mean you don't have a useful idea, but once again, you will probably have a hard time turning it into revenue.

Is My Product Disruptive?

If you have been around tech startups, this is a current buzz phrase. To be "disruptive" is to create something that shakes up an established marketplace or industry by doing something completely different. This can come in the form of displacing products, services, or even distribution in an industry where things have been fairly constant for a while. When I think of a mainstream disruptive startup, Uber always comes to mind. Uber did and continues to disrupt the cab industry. Another majorly disruptive technology is Airbnb. While people have certainly rented out their vacation homes or rented rooms since the inception of both, what Airbnb did was create a credible network to do so which disrupts the hotel industry. Later, when we get into venture capital, we will revisit why investors love disruptive technology.

Do I Enjoy This Product?

This isn't directly related to market viability, but it IS directly related to your ability to make it to the promised land. Starting a new business is a whole lot of work. Creating a *highly successful* business is even more work. Therefore, it is incredibly important that you enjoy or at least are interested in the industry and product. I will be the first person to tell you that large stacks of cash will make most things seem interesting. However, on the way to these large piles of cash is what feels like an infinite number of conversations about your products, services, website, or platform. If you don't have passion for what you are doing, then it's going to show and hinder your success. With GigaBook, I love what it does to help our users' businesses, but what I like even more is how it helps their lives. Online booking frees our users from the act of doing something that they usually don't enjoy. They seem to appreciate that perk more than the growth it creates in their businesses. This satisfaction makes it easy to talk about what we do.

Does My Product Have a Shelf Life or Is It Perishable?

If you are considering selling something that has a shelf life, or is perishable in some way, then you really need to dig deep when creating your plan. Selling this kind of product means that you will always be on the clock when it comes to selling it. And your distributors will be in the same boat. Since new businesses usually don't have a steady stream of revenue, you might find yourself sitting behind inventory that you have a hard time moving. This increases your risk—so much so that one wrong decision could potentially put you deep in a hole that might be really tough to escape.

Other Essential Things to Consider

Market viability is just one test your idea needs to pass before you should sink any money into your idea. Here are a couple other things that you must consider.

How Are You Planning on Marketing Your Product?

Are you a good salesperson? If not, then you better team up with someone who is. Sales and revenue are the lifeblood for your new business. Have you done research about the expenses that will be associated with advertising and marketing your product? In the beginning, you won't have a strong grasp of what produces returns compared to expenses. Then on top of this, there are nearly an unlimited number of ways to advertise your product. You really need to gain some understanding about what all things marketing could cost.

If your product or service requires a buy-in from other companies, then you need a plan for getting to the decision maker. This isn't easy. As a business owner, I can attest to the fact that I have become harder and harder to reach over the years. Business owners get bombarded daily with people trying to sell them stuff. It can be overwhelming. Most will just insulate themselves behind layers of employees or email addresses that are hard to locate. The bigger the company that you are trying to sell to the harder it is to locate the decision maker. Couple that with the fact that bigger companies move A LOT slower when it comes to making certain decisions. All of this is really important to consider when you think about how it impacts your current and future path to revenue.

IS MY IDEA AS GOOD AS I THINK IT IS?

Here is a moment where you really have to be honest with yourself. Lying to yourself about this can lead to financial ruin, years of wasted time and effort, or both.

If your idea, product, or service *did* in fact end up passing the market viability tests, then you may have a decent idea. If it struggled or failed the market viability tests, then you need to do some soul searching. It is really, really easy to over value our own opinions and ideas. The easiest way to figure out if your idea is great or not is to ask people. This can be tricky. In general, people won't want to tell you bad stuff largely because they want to be polite. So if you take this approach, you need to encourage anyone you speak with to be open with their feedback. And when they give it, LISTEN. Don't take anything personal, after all, you did ask. If your idea stinks, and they are telling you why, they might be doing you a HUGE favor by helping you understand that.

How Long Does It Take to Earn a Dollar?

If you randomly sat next to me on a flight, then engaged me in conversation about your great idea, I would invariably ask you the same question every time: What is your path to revenue? Yes, I'm bringing this up again because too many people don't give this enough thought. In fact, most hopeful business people I speak with don't seem to have considered it at all. Now, if you are creating a software platform or software as a service platform, your path to revenue is likely to be LONG. For some, even infinite. Why? Because you have to create something that others are willing to pay to use. It's that simple.

Many startup hopefuls are far too optimistic when it comes to how long it might take to collect one dollar. In a software marketplace flooded with products—many of which are "freemium," meaning you get some level of service without needing to pay at all—there is a lot of expectation from potential users when it comes to what they'll pay for. In fact, you will probably even find yourself surprised at how hard it can be to get people to sign up for your service when it's *free*.

When starting GigaBook, that was something we misjudged horribly. It took over a year before we collected our first dollar. Why? With other more complete products already out there, we found users saying things like "I need it to do X, Y, and Z. You only do X."

Do I Really Know What I Am Getting Myself Into?

Have you ever owned a business? If not, then let me tell you that you will go through many gut-wrenching moments. I'm probably understating that, too. Owning a business is intense and it is NOT for everyone. If you are already a high-anxiety person, beware. If you are someone who struggles to make decisions, then you might want to reconsider. Owning a business is HARD and it's STRESSFUL. It also comes with the need to make a whole lot of critical decisions.

As someone who owns and operates multiple businesses, I am going to try and convey some of what you are likely to experience as a business owner.

First off, if you aren't interested in being totally engulfed in work, don't start your own business. It doesn't always have to be like that, but the first phases of business ownership are just downright cruel when it comes to time commitment. In order to be successful, you aren't going to get away with a simple nine-to-five schedule, Monday through Friday. And that's the truth. Since you won't have a whole lot of resources starting out, you will find yourself doing A LOT of different things within your business, including the need to learn *how* to do a whole lot of new stuff. All time-consuming. Then on top of that, you are most likely going to need to work at the business during its normal operating hours. When I look back at my last ten years, I think it's fair to say that I worked about eighty hours a week along the way.

Next is the stress. This is hard to explain, because those around me say I seem to handle it well. I'm happy to hear this because I have definitely gone through times where I wanted to just close the door and quietly barf in my trash can. Now that you have that image in your head, let me ask, how well do you handle stress? If your answer is "poorly," then I strongly advise you to consider doing something else. Let me paint you a picture as to why. Think of how you would feel not knowing whether or not you were going to lose everything. I'm talking about your home, savings, credit, *all of it.* Then take that feeling and repeat it daily for a long duration of time. I am NOT being dramatic here either. I'm just trying to help you understand what you are in for.

Next let me ask, do you like being hungry? Of course nobody does. However, starting a new business is more or less going to guarantee that you go without in some regard. It may not manifest itself in the form of physical hunger, but it will come forth in other ways. Since your money will be tied up in your business, be prepared to make other sacrifices. If you aren't someone who's good at "bootstrapping" or living cheap, then you might want to learn to be. It's part of the process, so get ready.

The final question I have is, are you hungry enough? By this, I mean do you have a fire deep inside that drives you to win or be successful with whatever it is you're doing? Successful entrepreneurs usually do. It is my personal belief that you cannot create this relentless ambition. It just exists or happens to ignite in some of us. This means that you are willing to do what it takes to be successful, often at the expense of other things around you. Yes, that sounds a bit grim and that's because it is. This fire or drive to succeed has the ability to fuel what will become an obsession with being the best or winning. This, in turn, can keep you from other things in your life like friends, family, hobbies, and so on.

I know what I just laid on you wasn't coated with positivity. I am actually a really positive person, but that isn't what we are focused on. Remember, I'm trying to help you learn important lessons. It's okay if you now realize that what you were considering isn't the right idea for you. It's also okay if you realize that certain parts of this process are not what you are prepared for. My goal overall is to keep you safe from unnecessary loss and help you avoid some of the mistakes I made, or possibly avoided, along the way.

But if you are still on board with eyes open, let's get down to business.

A Conversation with
Matt Watson,
Founder of VinSolutions and
CEO/Founder of Stackify

Matt Watson, founder of VinSolutions and currently the founder and CEO of Stackify, is one of my favorite success stories. I'm going to leave the details of his story for you to learn during our conversation. What I will say is that Matt is without a doubt one of the smartest, tech-savvy people I have had the pleasure of getting to know. He has a way of clearly defining solutions and understanding the "now," while still having a firm grasp of the "later" when it comes to his businesses.

MATT DECOURSEY: What made you want to start VinSolutions?

MATT WATSON: I wasn't really setting out to start it. I was working at Sears selling computers. Any time someone came in to buy a computer, I would ask how it was to be used. One customer told me it was for his car dealership. And then he went on to tell me he had some software program and the guy who wrote it had gone off kilter. Now he was scared to death he was going to lose this database that the guy wrote. So I decided to help him out.

At the time, I was going to DeVry University but didn't have any professional experience doing development. I didn't really know what I was doing, but I ended up rewriting this whole program for the guy. I helped him over a couple years' time, just making little changes to it and whatever. So fast-forward back to your question. Randomly, some guy who worked for Autotrader.com was going around looking for a technical person to help him upload photos to the Internet and do some other technical stuff. He ran across the dealer I helped, who said, "Hey, you should talk to my friend Matt. He's a really smart tech guy. Maybe he can help you."

That's how it started. I sat down with the guy at an Applebee's and he described what he was trying to do, and I said, "I'll figure out how to do it." And that was it.

Were they your future business partners?

The second gentleman ended up being my partner. From the beginning, we were kind of 50/50 partners in the deal. The guy I met at Sears was never a partner; he was basically the friend who made the connection.

Just because I think it will amuse those of us who are over twenty-five, what kind of computers were you selling at Sears?

Most of them were Compaqs and Hewlett-Packards. Maybe a few Gateways.

Were the disks still floppy at that point or were we onto the hard floppy?

The best way I always remember this is we also sold digital cameras, and some of the digital cameras were the ones that still took three-and-a-half-inch hard floppies.

VinSolutions grew pretty fast. Did you take a particular approach to building it?

At the time, I was like twenty-two or twenty-three years old with no real business experience. I had no idea what I was doing. Really, I was just writing code. My business partner had some customers who we could sell to right away. I never really thought about it being a company. For me, it started out more like a side project. "Sure, I can help you do this, and if I make a few dollars from it, that's cool—we'll see what happens."

What made you realize this is something that could be big, as opposed to something that could be used by a couple of local car dealers?

I understood pretty fast the different kinds of technology products that existed which were similar to what we were trying to accomplish, and there really wasn't anything. Our original product was just a solution addressing a problem like *how do I take photos of cars, their pricing descriptions, and all that sort of stuff, and then syndicate it to other websites on the Internet?* As you can imagine, if you need to take five photos of the car and upload them to five or ten different websites, that's a pain. And then the next day, if you change the price of the car, you've got to change it on five or ten different websites. Ours was a really simple concept of just how to take and syndicate the data. We knew we had a product that filled a need, but when we started out in 2003–2004, we were probably a little ahead of the curve as far as people actually having digital cameras. We made a product that used Compaq iPAQs and stuff like PalmPilots. I even wrote a mobile app before mobile apps were a thing—a Windows CE mobile app that could take pictures of cars and then allowed you to input the car data. Back then, the little PalmPilot devices didn't have cameras in them, but they had little SD cards. They actually made a camera connected to an SD card that you could attach to the top of the PalmPilot. I remember it was like one megapixel photos and the photos were terrible.

That was back when a full megapixel was about as good as it got, right?

Yeah, and they were hideous. So we were kind of ahead of the times trying to help car dealers take photos of their cars and digitally upload them to the Internet. This was back in 2003–2004, and Autotrader.com was actually a new thing. Up until that time, the industry relied on print advertising. The whole movement to digital was just beginning.

What were some of the things that you had to learn really quickly?

I think the number one thing I learned over time is just how hard it is to really run a business. As a young company, we should have failed for a number of reasons—from the exit of my original business partner due to a whole bunch of issues to other business partners coming in, to facing more issues with one of those new partners. Originally, we thought we struck it rich when we reached a partnership with a giant company that was going to resell our software. Instead we spent a year or two trying to make that reseller partnership work and it went nowhere.

What did you learn from that? I had a similar experience with GigaBook. It wasn't two years, but I felt like we just spun our tires for four months. I realized I didn't move anything else forward.

I think one of the lessons is to let your success or failure remain in your own hands—especially when the company is young. If you don't know if the company is going to succeed or fail, you really don't want to turn that decision over to someone else. Gaining traction is something you should be in control of. Gain some traction, then make decisions like whether or not adding another sales channel makes sense. Depending on the type of product or service you are selling, that process can vary. For a software product like ours, we needed to perfect how we sold it to our customers. Turning that process over to someone else, and expecting them to do things we hadn't done yet, didn't work. Eventually, we woke up and decided that we had to take it all in our own hands. That is where our path to success began.

If you could fire up the time machine and go back and do something over, would that be it?

Not putting all of our eggs in one basket from a sales and a product development perspective. Despite all of the turmoil we had with business partners, the fact that we continued to do things to enhance the product was probably the reason we were ultimately successful. I managed to keep my head down through most of the surrounding turmoil, and eventually the product won. The product was good enough that we could sell it and it would be successful. And eventually, we figured out the best approach to selling within the industry.

As a programmer, you're ridden with failure until you find a solution. I understand that failure and the way you react to it has everything to do with what kind of success you find. Do you have any comments on that?

True. As a software developer, failure and problem-solving are really the nature of the job, right? You deal with trying things and they often don't work. Changing the code to fix the problem, that's what I do. Things break all the time and you've got to fix them. From that perspective, it's a pretty normal thing. Probably the biggest concern we ever had as a company was in 2008–2009. We were right in the thick of it when the economy went really bad. VinSolutions wasn't a big business yet, but we were definitely on the upswing. But then GM and Chrysler went bankrupt and then Ford closed a bunch of stores. We definitely couldn't raise capital at the time, which was a pretty scary moment for us as a company. We all just sat around kind of wondering what was going to happen the next day, the next month? What would be the repercussions of this?

It actually ended up being one of the most important things to ever happen to us because, when car dealers were making a lot of money, they didn't care what they were spending it on. Then all of a sudden, as the economy tightened up, everybody became a lot more scared about how they were spending their money. We were able to convince them that we could simultaneously save them money and help them transition from old newspaper and magazine-type advertising to digital advertising. And sell just as many cars. We were in the right place at the right time for that transition.

I tell people I don't believe in luck. It's more about preparation and opportunity meeting up. How do you feel about that?

Yeah.

Let me just back it up. What triggers that statement for me is when people say, "Wow, you've done well for yourself; you're really *lucky." Well, I didn't feel lucky when I was on my 98th hour last week.*

I wouldn't say anything we ever accomplished was due to luck—more so perseverance and overcoming all the obstacles and challenges of trying to run a business. The events in 2008–2009 with the economy actually helped us. We already had the product; we were prepared for it. We were doing the same thing we had always been doing—calling car dealers for the last two years and telling them, "Hey, you need to spend more of your money advertising online, and we can help you take pictures of your cars and help you build websites for your dealership. We can do all these things. Instead of spending twenty thousand dollars a month on a full-page ad in the local newspaper, why don't you spend that money on online advertising?" It was the same pitch we had the whole time. Previously they would say, "You know what? We're selling a lot of cars; we are not going to change what we're doing." Then all of a sudden, we call them up and they say, "That's a great idea. We'll save half that money and spend the other half on digital advertising. We'll buy your product to help." We were there making the same pitch except the market finally caught up to us. We were a little ahead of the times when it came to online advertising for dealers.

So being a technologist, you're obviously familiar with the term 'disruptive.' Do you think that what you were doing was disruptive at the time and that had something to do with the success of it?

VinSolutions was disruptive for a few reasons. One of them was that we combined different products into one platform, so our users—the dealers themselves—found a lot of value in one product. Their staff had one product to use rather than five products, and we had a bunch of cool features. Everything was tightly integrated. It was also 100 percent web-based. Some of our competitors were still selling their products with a three-year contract, and you had to buy a server and install it in the dealership. It was expensive and a pretty big commitment. So we came along with a low-cost product with no contract. We said, "Look, it's five hundred dollars a month. If you don't like it, you can cancel it next month and that's fine." And that was very disruptive to our competition. We literally put one of our competitors out of business. Totally toasted them because they were going to car dealers and asking them for fifty thousand-dollar contracts. It was pretty easy to get people to give us five hundred bucks for a one-month trial when our competition was asking for big, long-term deals. We were very disruptive from the perspective of being cloud-based, low priced, and no contract.

You and any other business that was operating in the cloud were first arrivals in a lot of ways.

Yeah, I'd say we were probably one of the earlier SaaS businesses that were 100 percent cloud-based. We had over a thousand clients that used our software and a really complicated data center to run all that stuff. It was a true Internet type business, but it wasn't business to consumer. It was business to business.

Even in 2017, it's hard to get people to understand some of this stuff. And this was all happening back in 2003–2012. Was that education even more of a challenge for the actual users? At that point, I don't imagine they would have had an IT guy.

Oh yeah. Our users were car salespeople or management on the sales side of the dealership. You had the old car dogs who had been there a long time, who really wanted nothing to do with technology. They were perfectly fine with doing everything the old way. These guys still don't use technology. They're more like "I sold fifty of those Chevy Malibus last year, and I know exactly what they're worth. And I don't need a damn book or computer to tell me." Those kinds of guys would never use our software.

But there is so much turnover in the car business. Most of our users were the salespeople, and those tended to be younger people. People who were in college or had dropped out of college and decided to go sell cars. They were more technology friendly. Some of them became the dealership's Internet manager, dealing with the online presence of the dealer, like selling cars online and dealing with Internet leads that came in. Over the years, the Internet became much more prevalent, and most of the dealers had at least one person who was the Internet sales manager.

If I look back at GigaBook and where it was going, the thing that I grossly underestimated was how difficult it is to get someone to change even if they really know they need to. We would get people on the phone who would say, "My business is a mess. My scheduling is a mess. I'm losing business every day. I need this badly." And I'd say, "You need to know that you're going to have to change the culture inside your business." And yet they wouldn't. They'd sign up and three days later they'd just be back to their old ways. It's easier to remain inefficient and continue sucking.

Yep. Absolutely.

So when you sold your company in May of 2011 for a lot of money, did you feel that changed others' perception of you? And their expectations?

It definitely changes the perception from people. But it didn't change me. I was never in it for the money. I didn't want my name in lights. To me, it was never about that. It was about "How do I help my customers? How do I solve the problem?" I'm just trying to make a business and make people happy. None of the rest of it really mattered. I would actually say the journey of building and growing the company was way more fun. Selling it was kind of anticlimactic for me. It was the end of a journey. I enjoyed the daily battle and climbing the mountain and building something. That part of the ride

155

was really fun. After you sell it, you sort of get off the rollercoaster and it's over. What do I do now?

One of the questions that I've received the most over the years (and I bet you get too) is people saying, "I want to make a lot of money. How do I do that?" And I always say don't focus on the money, focus on the process. I think that's what you just described. Be good at what you do.

You've got to solve a problem. So many people trying to start a business are simply trying to make a lot of money. But they've got to focus on a problem that people will pay them to solve. I still don't understand how Snapchat is worth so much more money than some of these other companies because they don't really solve a real problem.

There are so many different niches out there and ways to build a product and a business. Your biggest success is finding that niche and industry vertical that you have experience in, knowing how to do something differently (and better) than somebody else.

Recently I'm with my friend and he's like "Oh yeah, I know so and so, and so and so" and it's like this guy made all his money importing feathers from Africa. And this other guy did this crazy thing. And they are *all* just crazy things that nobody would ever think of doing to make a fortune. Everybody has this perception that you see somebody who's a millionaire with a big house and a Ferrari and you think that they must be a professional athlete or a celebrity or something, but they're not. They're usually entrepreneurs who have done things that you've never heard of, right? The public perception of that is all wrong. I feel bad for people who see me when I drive around in my car and they think I'm Kansas City Royals first basemen Eric Hosmer or something. It's just Matt Watson.

If you had to give advice to someone starting any business, what would it be?

I was watching *Planet Earth* the other day, and it was an episode about the jungle's complexity and all of the different species of animals that live there. They each manage to survive because they are the best at one specialized thing. And I think for *everyone* who wants to start a business, they've got to figure out what that *one thing* is for them. They can't be the king of the whole jungle. They need specialization, and they need to be the absolute best at that one thing.

Do you think you need to be the best at it right away, or can you become the best?

You at least need to go down the path where that one thing receives all your energy. One of the problems we had with Stackify was that I wanted to be the best at one thing, but my vision for that one thing was maybe a little too big. I really wanted to do four or five things and be really good at them all. In a lot of ways, we probably bit off more than maybe we should have. We got there, but it took us four or five years to reach. If we had done that *one* thing right off the bat, it might have taken us only a year or two. We would have been a best-in-class product in that one area. Maybe we were shooting for a bigger prize in the end, but it took way more time, effort, and capital to build the bigger vision and try to be the king of the whole jungle.

You gotta pick something you can actually accomplish and put all of your effort into if you want to be successful. And sometimes it's the simplest. I mean, there's a restaurant here in Kansas City that just opened and they only sell chicken fingers and fries. That's it. Why do they do that? I don't understand. You know I could go to Chick-fil-A. I could go somewhere else where they sell a bunch of different things. Or I can go to that restaurant where they sell one thing. Evidently, they must have really good chicken fingers.

I think that's my advice—you've gotta figure out what you're really really good at, and try and maximize that, before you get distracted doing other things.

I started Stackify to solve a lot of the challenges that I had as the founder and Chief Technology Officer of VinSolutions. At Vin, I had to deal with a large development team. We were rapidly growing and had lots of servers and developers. There were all sorts of problems. We didn't have the tools to really make the team more efficient or able to find and solve problems quickly, and it just was a lot of chaos. In general, software development is controlled chaos. But it wasn't very controlled. It was just chaos. The goal of Stackify was really to build developer tools that would control the chaos a little bit so the developers could be more self-service and have the tools they needed to understand if their applications were working—or how to fix problems that would come up. And that's what we built. Back to my previous analogy, it was complicated to build because it required so many different things to really work together.

Probably the easiest way to describe Stackify is if you've ever been on a website and it's really slow, or it's getting errors and you get frustrated with the website because you don't understand why it doesn't work—well, how does one solve that? Developers use tools like ours to know when and why that happens. So we are sort of like the black box on an airplane. We collect a whole lot of data that developers can use to understand why things are working the way they are and troubleshoot diagnostics.

What do you think the next twenty years will bring as far as technology, coding, or anything like that?

I think we are still in the middle of this industrial revolution, but it's the technology revolution. Be that with software, be that with robots, machine learning, artificial intelligence—the world is sort of the oyster of technicians at this point. There are so many different problems that can be solved. One of the things somebody told me that I always think about is this: Software developers really only do two things—they either make something go faster (by improving a business process or the speed of something) or they provide analytics (by providing knowledge or reporting about something). Those are two essential problems that virtually every business has and will always have. If you have one hundred employees who work in a call center, the owner of that call center is always going to be trying to figure out "How can I make my business more efficient? How can I have fifty people in my call center instead of one hundred? How can I get more insight into the type of people who are calling and the problems they're having?" Those are software development challenges that will always exist. And there will always be opportunities for entrepreneurs to solve those problems.

How can I help a business do things faster, more efficiently, or have more understanding about what it is they're doing? I think there's still a huge amount of opportunity out there for that. And it's in a lot of niches and industries that nobody's ever heard of. It's not creating the next Facebook. It's not creating the next Twitter or Snapchat, or Uber or any of those things. It's flight scheduling software for little airports, online scheduling software for a massage therapist, and so on. It's a lot of weird products and industries that nobody would ever know exist. *That's* where all the businesses live.

Final question. What would be the advice you would give to someone who's trying to get any scratch together for getting started?

Just from a capital perspective?

Anything. You're a guy with a laptop and a good idea. Where do we go from here?

I think the biggest thing you've got to be focused on is getting customers. Nobody these days is going to invest in any company that doesn't have revenue. It's very difficult to raise capital. And I see problems all the time where somebody with a smart idea wants to solve a technology problem, but they don't know anything about business. Or they want to solve a problem with technology, but they don't know anything about technology and they can't create the technology and so, therefore, they either have to go raise a bunch of capital, or spend a bunch of their own money hiring software developers and people to build the technology. Or they need to go find a cofounder, and what I tell them all the time is go find a cofounder who can become your business partner. Instead of trying to raise hundreds of thousands of dollars that you could be throwing away at some consulting firm that's going to write the software, just go find a cofounder and give them 20 percent of the company or whatever you would give the venture capitalist or investor. And have them build it. You don't need to raise the capital; instead just find a way to get it done.

Yeah. I get people who say "So did you program GigaBook?" and I reply "I don't write code; I write checks." But they're both pretty important. You don't always get one without the other.

You're the anomaly of somebody who's an entrepreneur that's had several technology ventures. But you're not a technologist and you've been able to figure out how to work with developers and the resources and fund those.

SECTION FOUR:

STICKING YOUR TOE IN THE POOL

CONGRATULATIONS ON making it this far. I certainly crushed the hopes and dreams of a few along the way. If that was you and you continued reading anyway, then you are stronger than you might believe yourself to be. The information in this final section is designed to help you learn more about what you need to do to start building your own Million Dollar Bedroom. I promise this section will feel a lot more uplifting. Think of the preceding reality check as the first days of Navy Seal training, where the instructors do nothing other than try to get you to quit. This is a necessary part of the process, largely because if you aren't ready or equipped for the road ahead, then you don't need to travel down that road.

Since we're on the subject of roads, let's start with the process of creating a roadmap. This includes the basic elements of a business plan but also some other forms of evaluation.

Creating a Cynically Optimistic Plan

If you fail to plan, then you plan to fail. Hopefully you've heard that somewhere else by now as I can't take credit for it. Regardless of where it came from, it's completely true. A thorough planning process is going to help you bring a lot of your ideas into reality. You start by creating a basic business plan. I stress the word "basic" here, as what follows is about as A-B-C or Business 101 as it gets. Still, this information isn't really up for debate when it comes to necessity or usefulness.

Whether you are seeking investment or not, this process yields both amazing insight and clarification. I wish I could tell you that I have some uniquely amazing business plan formula that, if followed, would result in you becoming rich. But it's a standard process that many, many before you have completed successfully; therefore, you can and must too. Let's break down the core elements you need to create a proper business plan.

WARNING: Some of this next part can be boring. Sorry, there really isn't a way to make financial projections captivating for all audiences. Despite that, it is ESSENTIAL. So don't take a nap through this part of class, or cut out while I'm not looking.

Executive Summary

This is your introductory statement. It should get right to the point about what you intend to do. Avoid statements like "We intend to bring forth the highest quality product possible while at the same time providing top-tier service." Okay, we all hope you do this; however, a statement like this does absolutely nothing to define your company as a whole. If you are seeking outside investment, I would avoid generic phrases like that altogether. Seasoned investors are immune to such statements.

Instead, get right to the point and list the basics stats and facts about your company. Think of this as looking at the back of a baseball card and reading a player's stats. If your business is brand new or still in the concept phase, then you won't have nearly as much information. List realistic opportunities, goals, and growth possibilities. Don't say that you expect to have a 90 percent market share within eighteen months of inception. If you have existing assets or investors for your new company, this is a good place to mention it.

Your grandmother probably told you that you only get one chance to make a first impression. Well, this is it. By the way, I'm supposed to remind you to wear clean underwear, which I hope you are doing anyway.

COMPANY DESCRIPTION

Complete this section using information that you gathered during your market viability testing. Briefly explain your products or services, highlighting the benefits they provide for existing or future customers.

After defining your basic product or service line, move on to stating who your intended target market and customers are. You should have this information readily available if you did the market viability research I suggested. Once again, mention some of the benefits that your product or service provides for your buyers. You don't need to get too deep with this information, as we are about to move on to a detailed market analysis.

The important thing to remember while completing this section of your plan is to focus on benefit statements. The effects and changes you provide for your buyers is what's important. If you create efficiency in their business, mention that. If you create a savings, certainly highlight that. Overall, if you do something better, faster, or cheaper, then this is the place to shine.

MARKET ANALYSIS

Now it's time to get scientific. Some of the things you have kept brief and to the point so far should now be expanded upon. Don't make guesses or assumptions here. Whether you are seeking outside money or not, it's just a bad idea. Instead, you need to work with precision and accuracy.

Start by defining your target market as a whole, and then break it down into smaller, more precisely defined groups. If you are planning on offering a product or service to distributors, be prepared to define who these distributors will need to market it toward.

LIST ALL COMPETITION. If you are seeking an investor and you don't do this, I can tell you right now that you aren't getting an investment. Without a doubt, you need to fully understand who you are up against and everything possible about them. This starts with their offerings in the market, but extends to their overall access to distribution and resources. Are they a huge company or are they small? There is a big difference in the type of competition that you are likely to get from either.

The best business people and salespeople in the world understand their competitors' products nearly as much as their own. Without doing so, you can't really figure out ways to stand out and be better. Trust me, your competitors are going to get to know your business pretty well.

Now that you have defined your product offerings as well as the competitors', it's time to figure out which portion of the market you can "reasonably" obtain and how long it might take to do so. You need to thoroughly list your plan for doing this, too. You can't just say you are going to do it.

After you have detailed *how* you are planning on gaining market share, you can then explain and demonstrate your pricing strategy and the gross margins that might possibly come with your sales.

To finalize this section, if there is anything blocking your path to revenue, it should be clearly stated here as well. In seeking investment, you need to be transparent about this; not doing so is unethical and could lead to big problems for you later. Some of these restrictions might include licenses or permits you need and don't have, or other types of regulatory issues that could possibly prevent your plan from unfolding.

ORGANIZATION AND MANAGEMENT

Okay, enough of that other stuff! Let's get into the people part of your plan. This is another key ingredient if you are seeking investors. Seasoned investors and firms look just as much at the key players in a company as they do at the idea. Why? Because a track record of success (with some failures along the way) says a lot about you. So why mention failure? Because you often learn more from your failures than your successes. Some investors might not like giving a large bankroll to someone who *hasn't* failed. It's due to these individuals having a somewhat bulletproof feeling about them. Failure teaches you humility, and fast!

Before you start selling yourself and all of the things you are amazing at, first visit the basic structural details of your company. This includes the type of entity you have created, meaning an LLC, corporation, or other. After defining the entity, you will then need to clearly outline the ownership situation in the company. Meaning, you will need to define and state who owns what, as well as their involvement in the company both now and in the future. If you have already taken on other investors or accumulated debt, this needs to be clearly stated here, too.

Now that you've outlined the stats and structure, it's time to get into who YOU are. This means yourself and any other talent you have onboard. Don't be shy here either. If you are top notch at something or you bring experience that is hard to find, MENTION IT! This is exactly what an investor will be looking for.

To round out this section, state who is currently a member of your board of directors if you have one. A board of directors is established in most companies that have shareholders in order to create a governing body that controls the company as a whole. If you aren't familiar with how this works, then you need to start googling and understand it before you agree to anything with others. Just remember, having an all-star team is desirable, so do what you can to create one.

SERVICE OR PRODUCT LINE

Even though you have already mentioned parts of this previously, it's a good idea to create a section of your plan dedicated to this topic. This allows for a truly detailed explanation of your service or product. If you have patents or plan to file them, this is where you can clearly define your plans. If your plan will require research and development (R&D), then you will need to detail that here as well. Make sure you truly understand these costs before presenting your plan to an investor. Giving inaccurate projections for R&D or production costs is a no-no. If your investor does their due diligence and discovers you are wrong here, it's likely they will just assume all of the other information in your plan is also incorrect. This results in no investment.

SALES AND MARKETING PLAN

We got into this earlier, so if you did the previous projections I suggested, then you should have some of this information already. This is where you detail your plan for getting your product out into the market. For me, this is the greatest part of the plan, or at least the most fun. It's where the real action takes place.

When creating a sales and marketing plan, you need to clearly define the medium you plan on using. By this, I mean what is your sales vessel? Is it advertising? Is it actual salespeople? Maybe both. In my opinion, a great sales and marketing plan includes a primary and secondary plan. This shows that you are ready to adjust or adapt if the primary plan doesn't give the results you are looking for.

In addition to listing a primary and secondary plan, you also need to detail what your plan is when it comes to learning from your customer and client input. Meaning, how do you plan on utilizing your sales and marketing expenses to also benefit the company in the form of valuable feedback? This is basically figuring out why people aren't buying from you, then how you plan on using that input to fix the problem.

Now that you have covered the details of your marketing plan, you need to make sure that you clearly establish what your cost or budget is for it. In addition, you need to know and understand your cost of acquiring business. You can absolutely spend an infinite amount of money on advertising; it's endless. So what you need to do is place a cap on the budget as a whole then spread this budget out over a series of months. To finalize your plan, state what you reasonably expect to gain from your sales and marketing expenses, both now and long term. This isn't something that can always be detailed accurately, as there are too many variables to hit the bulls-eye every time. Just be reasonable with your estimates.

Funding Plan or Request

Now on to the meat and potatoes: FUNDING. Whether you seek outside money or not, this is where plans live or die. Why? Because running out of money is bad! Businesses fail every day due to poorly estimating how long their existing funds will last compared to the true path to revenue. When it comes to estimating expenses, common wisdom is you should take what you think you need and DOUBLE it. That isn't good enough for me. I want you to TRIPLE it. Remember, I'm here to hopefully help you avoid expensive pitfalls.

This approach will also go a long way with potential investors. They want to see that your calculations and estimates include wiggle room. The reason it is needed is because you often times have no clue what you really need, until the time you need it. With any new business—no matter how much you anticipate the future and its needs—you just never really know.

I want to re-emphasize this critical point. OVERESTIMATE YOUR EXPENSES COMPARED TO CAPITAL! Underestimating how long your cash will last, or being seriously wrong about when cash will come in, is one of the most common mistakes that startup founders and new business owners make. As a result, many find themselves in a crippling situation. The poor planning leaves them either out of money and unable to continue or forced to sell off large amounts of equity long before it had realized its full potential. Either way isn't good.

FINANCIAL PROJECTIONS

Up until now, we have thrown around a lot of information. Some of that information was easy to project, predict, or maybe even guess. Well, we aren't going to be anything other than realistic and scientific when it comes to financial projections. This is the hardest part of any business plan for most. Those who don't consider themselves "math or finance people" might be cringing about this part already. Regardless of where you sit when it comes to math skills, this is something that you really must try and figure out. That being said, I'm not an accountant or mathematician, but I can certainly create financial projections.

Creating basic financial projections is actually a pretty easy process. Start with a blank spreadsheet and then create a column for which the cells contain the months of your future timeline. Next, create an adjacent column for the monthly revenue estimations. Make sure these numbers *very reasonably* represent what your initial efforts should, could, or might create in terms of revenue. Now after twelve months' worth of revenue

174

estimates, run a quick auto sum and see what you come up with. Congratulations! You just created your first revenue projection.

This is the simplest way to start modeling your future revenue. Yes, there are way more complex ways of doing this, but let's start here. Within this elementary model, you can now make your first comparison of revenue versus expenses. Doing this creates the first projection of your future business's profit or loss in the first year.

Once again, what I just explained is without a doubt the simplest way to create a revenue projection. Using this and playing with its numbers will give you a better idea of where you need to be in order to survive. I have used this same simplistic modeling format to quickly determine the overall viability of my own business ideas or those being pitched to me.

Here are a few things to consider when creating your first financial projection:

- Growth is usually slow in the beginning.
- The idea that your revenue growth will be linear is flawed. Meaning, it won't come at the same percentage of growth monthly.
- Unexpected things happen, meaning growth isn't a guarantee. Plan for setbacks.
- It is smart to create *multiple* projections models— bad, good, and great.

- Don't be overly optimistic about your revenue growth, as that leads to false confidence. If any time is best to be a realist, this is it.

EXPENSE PROJECTIONS

While revenue projections are about as accurate as a blind archer, your expense projections can be somewhat precise. Keep in mind that this part of the planning process is one that deserves as much or more attention as the other parts of your planning. I like to say that saving money equals making money. On the flip side, spending more means you are making less.

With expense projections, you have quite a bit to consider when it comes to the scalability and growth of your enterprise. An easy way to create a projection or idea of expense scalability is to start with your most basic revenue versus expense model. After you feel fairly comfortable with what you came up with, you can then measure the percentage each expense has compared to revenue.

Example: If $100,000 in revenue requires $10,000 in labor, then your labor expense is 10 percent of revenue. So we can estimate that $300,000 in revenue might require $30,000 in labor.

Is this approach accurate? Nope. Nothing with the word "projection" next to it is. However, it's better than guessing. It's also important to give consideration to other growth-related expenses. Here are a few items to consider:

- New equipment required for larger operation
- Additional accounting expense
- Increase in accounts receivables
- Technology needs

Estimating Labor and Wage Expenses

In most businesses, wages and labor is the largest expense. With that, there are expenses associated with having employees: taxes, payroll-related expenses, and benefits are the most common. When it comes to the estimation of labor and wage-related expenses, I like to use what is referred to as "Burden Rate." This term is very appropriately named, as these expenses really can feel burdensome. I like to use 20 percent as my default number when creating this estimate. Yes, that is correct. You can probably expect to spend somewhere near this amount for every dollar you pay out in wages.

Another important thing to plan for is the fact that ALL of your expenses will rise yearly with inflation. You can expect everything your business buys to cost 3–4 percent more next year. In addition, your employees will cost more too. So if you are creating a 3–5-year plan or projection, you need to account for this.

Appendix, Containing Examples or References

Congratulations! If you made it this far with your business plan, then you made it through all of the tough parts. In this final part of your plan, attach any supporting materials like graphs, charts, or other support material that you might have referenced in your plan but chose not to display in full.

A Final Note for Those Seeking Investment

If you are seeking outside investment, be sure your business plan is remarkably complete and presentable. Quadruple check all parts of your plan. Give it to several other people to read if you need to. Take the time to work on your layout and presentation. All of this speaks volumes about how you will run your business in the eyes of investors. If your plan is poor and incomplete (or filled with typos), then the way you run your business might easily be as careless. Put yourself in the shoes of your potential investor. If someone came to you with a sloppy plan, would you feel excited about giving them a large chunk of your money? I wouldn't either.

Important Decisions That Can't Be Undecided

In the process of creating your plan, you clearly detailed the structure of your business. It is important that these decisions be made with some kind of logic. As I shared with you early in the book, when I started my first company, I sold off a large chunk of it to an inactive business partner. At the time, that seemed fine. In fact, it was more than fine—it was necessary in order to grow.

However, I later realized that what I had done to satisfy the immediate, in turn, really cost me in the long run. Therefore, view these decisions from a practical standpoint. Before you make any big decisions, it's best to consult with a licensed professional about what your state allows and what might be best for you overall.

Determining Equity and Roles

One of the most hotly contested topics when starting a business with partners, or with the help of an investor, is the division of equity. Many people seem to toss equity around as if there is a bountiful supply of it. Well, there isn't. It is finite. Sure, certain arrangements and provisions can allow for ownership to change hands in certain ways; however, there is only 100 percent of total ownership in your business.

A recent situation comes to mind. Somewhat often I have people seeking my free advice about some idea they have. Just to make sure it's not the next big thing, I usually listen, but only up to a certain point when I realize that it's not for me. That being said, these folks made it all of the way to the conference room. After I began listening to the rest of their presentation, I asked the question about ownership. What happened next really blew me away.

Over the next ten minutes, I watched four people throw equity numbers around in a way that had absolutely no real logic attached. One partner somehow went from 25 percent down to 5, or maybe 8, I'm not sure, as it was pretty hard to keep up with. Then I asked what kind of investment they sought. I was told a large number with a small percentage. Overall, the valuation came up to over a million dollars, and for a company that hadn't even been formed yet. Sadly, this isn't uncommon.

So why does this occur? There are a few likely culprits. The first one being inexperience. That was the issue I once had. Next in line is misunderstanding the value of your company, both now and later. Together these factors create a really regrettable mix. The value of a business comes from either its potential profit or its actual profit (for businesses already in motion). Using certain multipliers based on industry and then profit or sometimes revenue, a value can be determined. If you are pre-revenue, then your value is just a guess. It is most likely small and the risk is high—at least that is how your investors are likely to view it.

Funding, Funding, Funding

These words pretty much sum up what most people with an idea for the next big thing need. Unless you have already found financial success through whatever means, then you too will utter these words.

Finding money isn't easy. Period. Most people don't have enough of it to give you what you need, and those who do usually aren't willing to part with it on a whim. What you are likely to find is a long series of "No's" when it comes to obtaining funds. In addition, I want you to act responsibly when it comes to asking people for money. Doing so puts them in the exact same boat as you when it comes to success. By this, I mean that your failure could have a profound impact on their situation as well. As a result, you might find yourself in a tense or regrettable situation with those you care about the most. I'm NOT saying that you shouldn't turn to those around you first—in fact, that is what most people do. What I AM saying is that you should make sure that if they do choose to invest money into your project, then they do so with a full understanding of what they are getting into, when and how that money might be returned to them, and anything else that is relevant to the overall success of your business.

The VC Experience

For those not familiar, the term "VC" stands for venture capitalist. A VC is usually either a firm or an individual that specializes in funding businesses at various stages of the growth process. There are a lot of these firms and individuals out there; however, getting an investment from them is actually quite difficult. Why is it so hard? The first reason is that these firms are usually buried with requests for funding, so based on numbers alone, you are already looking at an uphill climb. Next, money available to lend or invest needs to be done so wisely. Since VCs most likely have quite a bit of experience, they understand the odds. Those odds being that you are more likely to fail than succeed. Doing so with their money is exactly what they need to avoid. In addition, in my communication with those associated with VC firms, it is pretty common for them to have their investments stuck in various companies. By stuck, I mean that they invested in a company that isn't really failing but also isn't succeeding. Therefore, they can't exit the situation and also might not want to invest further. Without being able or willing to do either, they are stuck in a situation of not having funds readily available.

Now that you know what a VC is, let me prep you for the total experience. The process of raising money is a long and tiresome one. If you are easily discouraged or offended, then you are doomed. Even the best businesses, ideas, and platforms run into huge amounts of rejection along the path toward funding. If you DO manage to get a response and a meeting, then make sure you are prepared. These people speak in terms of numbers, not just optimism. So base your presentation on logic. Be prepared to fully detail *how* and *when* they might possibly see their money returned to them. Most VC firms are interested in helping recipients of their funding find hyper growth, and then they want to experience an exit. Meaning, they want to sell their stake in the business off to an acquiring entity for a larger sum than they invested. So speak their language and be prepared to explain how you are going to help them accomplish that goal.

Smart Money vs. Not-So-Smart Money

On the most basic level, money doesn't have a brain. But when an investor is attached to that money, it certainly does. While funding is great, should you find yourself in a situation where someone is about to write you a check, you need to consider a few things. What kind of new responsibility and expectations are you about to have? Most investors or VCs aren't just going to hand you a check and then hope you call them in a year letting them know how successful you have become. In fact, you should expect quite the opposite. You are about to have a new level of "fiduciary" or financial responsibility. Sometimes this will require additional expense in the form of bookkeeping and accounting processes that you might not currently be using. These come from the newfound need to be fully accountable for where you spend money and where you take it in.

Okay, back to why money can actually be smart. An investor can provide cash, credit, advice, or connections. A "Smart Money" investor can provide more than one of these. An example would be someone who has the ability to get you or your business in front of new and exciting opportunities for growth. Since this investor would have a vested interest in your success, it would be in their best interest to help you find these opportunities. Now let's say that your idea or business is strong enough to garner multiple funding options. First off, congratulations on that, but now you will have a decision make. Without knowing more, I can't tell you which to choose. The majority would say the "Smart Money" is the right move in most spots, however, that is up to you to determine.

You Will Determine Your Own Outcome

I don't believe in luck. I believe that what most refer to as luck is just preparation and opportunity at an intersection. I say this a lot, and people ask, "What about winning the Powerball?" Okay, you were prepared when you bought the ticket; then the opportunity occurred when they drew the numbers. It is all up to YOU for the most part. There are certainly other factors at play, some more controllable than others. The one factor that you can certainly control is yourself—your own actions, decisions, and input into your business.

During the timeline of my own story, I often worked hours that some would consider cruel. I delayed my own access to certain comforts that I could have easily had in order to further my business interests. At times, I even sacrificed my own sense of life-balance—all for the sake of achieving my goals. I don't have any regrets for doing so. That all being said, it *is* important that you work within a reasonable set of goals, expectations, and risk. What might work and feel comfortable for you, might not be ideal for another. In the end, it is important that you do what feels comfortable, reasonable, and responsible when it comes to your unique situation.

I sincerely hope that some of the lessons I learned along the way prove helpful to you, and that they save you quite a bit of money as well.

Now get started! You've got a lot of work to do.

AFTERWORD:

AT THIS POINT IT'S UP TO YOU

So what do you think? I'm sure quite a few readers didn't make it to the end of the book. If you did, then, at a minimum, you find business and entrepreneurship interesting. Or maybe you liked the story—hopefully both.

As I wrap this up, the one thing I have to say is YOU have the ability to write your own story of success. My wish is that through reading mine you also understand that the road to success is invariably littered with failures too. How you react to those failures has a lot to do with whether or not you succeed. Be positive, hardworking, and eager to become a better version of yourself, and your chances of success will multiply. As a bonus for making it this far, I'm going to list several ideas and ways for you to get started. Yes, I know in the first moments of the book I stated that I couldn't give you the blueprint for success. But I never said that I wouldn't give you a few pointers. After spending all of this time together, it's my pleasure.

Ways You Can Make Money Online

- Affiliate Marketing
- Content or Video Production
- Product Resale
- Providing Virtual Services
- Programming or Project Management

For more information, updates, and new content, visit MattDeC.com.

GLOSSARY

affiliate marketing—a performance-based marketing system where the sponsoring business rewards its marketers based on traffic, sales, or leads generated.

barrier to entry—factors that limit or prevent competition from entering an industry. Usually related to high startup costs, but also can be related to technology, experience, or other niche factors.

Black Hat SEO—the use of SEO (Search Engine Optimization) tactics that only relate to gaining favorable search results, often times in violation of search engine terms of service or guidelines.

board of directors—a group of individuals who act as representatives of the stockholders of the company, making decisions on policies, course of action by the company, and other important decisions.

burden rate—an estimation of labor and wage-related expenses you can expect to spend for every dollar you pay out in wages.

burn rate—the rate at which a business or startup spends money (or venture capital) over and above income. Used to determine how long capital will last before being totally exhausted.

business entity—the chosen form a business takes either at inception or the form it becomes later. The type of entity chosen/used determines several other factors such as taxes, liability, or other practices.

business plan—a written statement of goals and the approach that will be used to achieve those goals in a new or existing business. Used for purposes of planning new operations or obtaining investment resources.

C-corporation—a business that is taxed separately from its owners or shareholders. C-corporations are usually larger companies with multiple owners and shareholders.

cease and desist letter—the first step in asking an individual or company to stop performing or engaging in some form of activity. The purpose of the letter is to threaten further legal action should they not stop performing said actions.

chargeback—a disputed charge by a credit card holder. Often used to recover funds associated with fraudulent purchases, or where the buyer is not satisfied with the services or goods received.

charge card—a type of credit card requiring full repayment within a given period. Charge cards are different from standard credit cards that allow payment over time with accrued interest also being charged.

comingling—to mix personal and professional funds together, making it difficult to determine which funds are which.

company description—part of a formal business plan where the vision and direction of the company are explained. This allows potential investors and partners to gain a better understanding of the company's broader objectives.

consignment—to sell your goods through another's sales channels. An example is a "consignment shop" that takes products and sells them on behalf of various sellers. A consignment seller will only be paid upon the sale of the item in most cases.

cost of goods (COG)—direct costs associated with acquiring or producing goods that are sold by a company. A number of factors are used to determine COG. Please refer to whatever accounting standards and guidelines you use to accurately determine costs.

crapplications—any resume, job application, or form of communication inquiring about contracts or employment that is clearly done poorly, unprofessionally, or in a way that indicates the sender is not at a level of competence necessary to perform on a high level.

disruptive innovation—anything that creates a new market or changes the way existing markets, industries, firms, or networks operate.

double taxation—refers to taxes paid twice on the same source of income. For example, a business pays tax on its profits, then when those profits are distributed to shareholders, they also pay taxes on those distributions.

equity—a security or anything representing an ownership interest in a business. Can also be used in reference to the plus or minus value one holds on something of value.

executive summary—part of a formal business plan that summarizes longer sections of the overall business plan. Can also be used to quickly describe the managers in a business.

financial projections—a forecast of future revenue, expenses, and profitability. Created using historical data coupled with future expectations.

funding plan—a written document that defines an organization's need for, then potential use of, funding over a period of time.

grassroots marketing—refers to marketing efforts NOT associated with the purchase of advertising, but instead the use of time, effort, or existing resources in order to gain exposure for one's business or idea. Sometimes called guerilla marketing.

gross margin—the difference between revenue and cost of goods sold.

leverage—the use of OPM (Other People's Money) to achieve financial gain. Also the ratio of debt compared to the company's overall value. On a basic level, when you purchase a home only to rent it out, you are leveraging the bank's money for your long-term gain.

limited liability company (LLC)—a business entity that allows for a pass-through tax structure while at the same time allowing for similar protections from liability as corporations. LLCs are NOT corporations.

long tail marketing—attempting to gain sales in less competitive areas of marketing or advertising. Aiming efforts away from the mainstream and into smaller niche focuses.

market analysis—an assessment of the size of a given market, both for overall volume and total value. Also takes into consideration economic trends, patterns, competitive elements, and comprehensive environment.

market viability—evaluation of overall market demand, competition, and whether or not a product will be sellable, sustainable, and/or profitable within a market.

minimally viable product (MVP)—the most basic state of a product where enough features exist to allow for gathering valid user input and data that can be used to further develop said product.

non-compete agreement—a contract disallowing one or more parties from competing against each other in similar projects or professions. This is an agreement usually requested by employers.

off-page SEO—the variables not seen on a webpage that a search engine does see that help determine your search results.

offshore labor—to hire employees or contractors in a country not the same as your own or your company's.

organization and management—part of a formal business plan that clearly defines and profiles the managers of the existing or proposed company.

outsource—to hire employees or contractors outside of your company's.

page description—also referred to as meta tag description. This is a short snippet of text used to summarize a web page's content.

page source—sometimes referred to as source or document source. This is the HTML code or source code associated with a web page.

page title—HTML code that appears in the title bar or tabs of a browser.

partnership—an arrangement between two or more parties to share the profits and liabilities associated with a business venture.

pass-through entity—a business entity that allows for the profits and losses to pass through to the owners' income tax returns. This means the entities themselves are not taxed. Sole proprietorships, partnerships, LLCs, and S-corps are all examples of pass-through entities.

path to revenue—the course of action a company chooses that defines how quickly or when they will record their first or recurring revenue.

point of sale (POS)—the time and place where a transaction occurs. Also a common term for the actual terminal, software, or device used to record, track, and facilitate a transaction.

profit margin—the amount of revenue that exceeds costs in a business.

product line—a group or series of products that exist under a single brand or sold by the same company.

purchase order (PO)—a document issued from a buyer to a seller indicating the intent to purchase and also defining quantity, price, and description of the products or services the buyer would like to purchase, along with any additional terms such as the number of days until payment is rendered.

receivable (also known as accounts receivable or A/R)—a claim for payment held by a business that has already supplied goods or services to another business.

research and development (R & D)—work directed towards the innovation or improvement of products or processes.

sales and marketing plan—a strategy or process for creating new business, adding clients, or building a brand.

scalability—the ability or ease at which a business operation or components are able to change in size, functionality, or other ability to adapt to changes. Can also take into consideration the speed at which change can occur.

S-corp—a tax election allowing for pass-through income to occur, thus preventing instances of double taxation.

search engine optimization (SEO)—the process or techniques associated with maximizing traffic to a website through search engine results.

services—doing work for another party for a fee.

service fee—an extra charge that is assessed over and above the service provided.

shareholders—the owners of a business, usually determined through issuance of stock or other securities that determine the value of the business.

sole proprietorship (also known as a sole prop)—a type of business entity that is run by one person where no legal distinction exists between the owner and the business.

target customer or **target market**—a group of clients or customers that a business is aiming to reach with marketing efforts.

Tax ID Number (or Taxpayer Identification Number [TIN])—an identifying number issued by the IRS or Social Security Administration that is used for various reporting and tracking purposes associated with the business.

turn ratio—a formula used to determine how many times a company's inventory is sold and replaced over a period of time. There are multiple formulas for determining turn ratio; the most common is dividing net sales by average inventory value.

venture capitalist (VC)—an investor who provides cash, connections, or other resources needed for a small business to expand and grow in exchange for partial ownership.

White Hat SEO—use of search engine optimization techniques that focus more on human audiences than an attempt to gain search position. These techniques also comply with search engine guidelines and terms of service.

ACKNOWLEDGMENTS

How do you acknowledge people who you don't directly name in your book? I'm going to try!

THANK YOU TO EVERYONE WHO PLAYED A ROLE IN THIS STORY. You know who you are.

I'd like to thank my wife, Jill. Without you, this story wouldn't have happened. You don't give yourself enough credit, you really should! You truly are a rock star!

Thank you to "The Intern." We miss working with you buddy! Without you, I'm not sure this story turns out so well. The fact that we once had to force you to take a vacation really says a lot about what an amazing part of the team you were.

I'd also like to say thanks to all of the friends, family, and neighbors that, in some way, at some time, helped.

I would without a doubt like to send my love to all of my Cebu City, Philippines staff! Thank you so much. Once again, this story probably isn't the same without all of you. I feel that we got to change each other's lives in such a positive way.

Thanks to John Berman; GigaBook wouldn't have made it to where it is without you. You truly are what would happen if R2-D2 and C3-PO had a baby.

While I didn't mention this part in the book, I'd like to thank the freaking chipmunk that lived under the floor of the Million Dollar Bedroom for what seemed like forever. You made us really want to do well enough to get out of that bedroom!

Then we get to Patrick Price, who I still consider to be the world's BEST editor! Since I now know more than one editor, this statement should mean more compared to the last book.

To Krista Vossen, thank you for making my books look so pretty and original—and for putting up with me telling you that things looked crooked when they weren't and I really just needed sleep.

To Sarah Cisco, thank you for the expert copyediting.

For those who had conversations with me for this book, thank you! Hopefully you did it because you wanted to and not so I would quit calling.

Lastly, I'd like to thank all of the amazing peers and positively awesome people I met, did business with, and learned from over the course of this story. There are seriously too many of you to name here, but you know who you are. So many of you helped me spark the next wild innovation, or possibly helped me pick myself up after a failure. Thank you!

ABOUT THE AUTHOR

Matt DeCoursey is the author of *Balance Me* and founder and CEO of GigaBook, a cloud-based appointment-booking platform, which has the ability to provide utility to millions of small- and medium-sized businesses. He also owns and operates other businesses. He lives in Kansas City with his wife, son, and daughter. Visit Matt at www.mattdec.com for more information, ideas, and inspiration.